PIZZA, PASTA & RISOTTO

180 BEST-LOVED RECIPES FROM YOUR ITALIAN TRATTORIA

Easy Italian classics for every day and special occasions, with step-by-step instructions and over 200 fabulous photographs   Edited by Jeni Wright

southwater

Publisher's Note:
Although the advice and information in this book are believed to be accurate and true at the time of going to press, neither the authors nor the publisher can accept any legal responsiblity or liability for any errors or omissions that may be made.

Front cover: Rigatoni with Winter Tomato Sauce, see page 6

Ethical Trading Policy
At Anness Publishing we believe that business should be conducted in an ethical and ecologically sustainable way. As a publisher, we use a lot of wood pulp to make high-quality paper for printing, and that wood commonly comes from spruce trees. We are therefore currently growing more than 750,000 trees in three Scottish forest plantations: Berrymoss (130 hectares/ 320 acres), West Touxhill (125 hectares/305 acres) and Deveron Forest (75 hectares/185 acres). The forests we manage contain more than 3.5 times the number of trees employed each year in making paper for the books we manufacture.
Because of this ongoing ecological investment programme, you, as our customer, can have the pleasure and reassurance of knowing that a tree is being cultivated on your behalf to naturally replace the materials used to make the book you are holding.
Our forestry programme is run in accordance with the UK Woodland Assurance Scheme (UKWAS) and will be certified by the internationally recognized Forest Stewardship Council (FSC). The FSC is a non-government organization dedicated to promoting responsible management of the world's forests. Certification ensures forests are managed in an environmentally sustainable and socially responsible way. For further information about this scheme, go to www.annesspublishing.com/trees

This edition is published by Southwater Books
Southwater is an imprint of Anness Publishing Ltd
Hermes House, 88–89 Blackfriars Road,
London SE1 8HA
tel. 020 7401 2077; fax 020 7633 9499

www.southwaterbooks.com; www.annesspublishing.com

If you like the images in this book and would like to investigate using them for publishing, promotions or advertising, please visit our website www.practicalpictures.com for more information.

Publisher: Joanna Lorenz
Editorial Director: Helen Sudell
Project Editor: Rosie Gordon
Production Controller: Mai-Ling Collyer
Contributors: Catherine Atkinson, Angela Boggiano, Carla Capalbo, Jacqueline Clark, Maxine Clark, Carole Clements, Roz Denny, Joanna Farrow, Christine France, Silvano Franco, Sarah Gates, Shirley Gill, Norma McMillan, Sue Maggs,, Elizabeth Martin, Annie Nichols, Jenny Stacy, Liz Trigg, Laura Washburn, Steven Wheeler, Jenny White and Jeni Wright

Previously published as part of a larger volume, *500 Italian Recipes* by Jeni Wright

Notes

Bracketed terms are intended for American readers.

For all recipes, quantities are given in both metric and imperial measures and, where appropriate, in standard cups and spoons. Follow one set, but not a mixture, because they are not interchangeable. Standard spoon and cup measures are level. 1 tsp = 5ml, 1 tbsp = 15ml, 1 cup = 250ml/8fl oz. Australian standard tablespoons are 20ml. Australian readers should use 3 tsp in place of 1 tbsp for measuring small quantities of gelatine, flour, salt etc. American pints are 16fl oz/2 cups. American readers should use 20fl oz/ 2.5 cups in place of 1 pint when measuring liquids.

Electric oven temperatures in this book are for conventional ovens. When using a fan oven, the temperature will probably need to be reduced by about 10–20°C/20–40°F. Since ovens vary, you should check your manufacturer's instruction book for guidance.

The nutritional analysis given for each recipe is calculated per portion (i.e. serving or item), unless otherwise stated. If the recipe gives a range, such as Serves 4–6, then the nutritional analysis will be for the smaller portion size, i.e. 6 servings. Medium (US large) eggs are used unless otherwise stated.

Important: pregnant women, the elderly, the ill and very young children should avoid recipes using raw or lightly cooked eggs.

Contents

Introduction

Italy is a country of great diversity. Rolling miles of rural hills, spotted with ancient walled towns, give way to sophisticated cities such as Milan and Rome. In every area there are eateries that celebrate local ingredients and traditional cooking, often enhancing age-old recipes with modern twists. With its sun-drenched farmland and sweet, succulent fruits and vegetables, Italy produces food and wine that is deservedly famous, and has been adopted all over the world.

Each region has nurtured distinct cultural differences, still present in the culinary practices today. Despite globalization and mass-marketing, traditional foods are still central to the identity of each region. This is partly due to the way in which recipes are learned: orally passed from generation to generation, and rarely written down in cookbooks, they survive in families for years with little or no change made to them. A great deal of Italian food comes from this "contadino", or peasant, heritage.

Some of Italy's best known dishes are pizza, pasta and risotto. Popular the world over, they are known as good, carbohydrate-

Above: Margherita pizza is an unbeatable classic.

rich and convenient foods. Many of these recipes can be prepared quickly and economically, and the best dishes marry fresh ingredients with simple cooking techniques. Tender grains and pasta ribbons are tossed with herbs and olive oil, and aromatic sauces can often be assembled in the time it takes pasta to boil. Pizza breads are dressed with the best tomato sauces, cheeses and meat or vegetables, before being baked to perfection. Rice cooked in stock, with a handful of wild mushrooms or fresh rocket and a grating of Parmesan, makes a magnificent dish.

The Italian diet, which is high in vegetables and carbohydrates and low in animal fat, is a healthy one. It also tastes exceptionally good. Italian cooking is based on the creative use of fresh, seasonal ingredients. Vegetables and herbs play central roles in almost every aspect of the menu. In the markets, there is a sense of anticipation at the beginning of each new season, heralded by the arrival, on beautifully displayed stalls, of the year's first artichokes, olives, chestnuts and wild mushrooms. Seasonal recipes come to the

Left: A simple sprinkling of herbs and grated Parmesan cheese complements fresh ravioli.

fore and make the most of the produce. Many of the treats once considered exotically Mediterranean are now readily available in the markets and supermarkets of most countries. For example, fennel and aubergine (eggplant), peppers, courgettes (zucchini) and radicchio are often used in pasta sauces, risottos and pizzas.

When filling your refrigerator, look for the freshest possible fruits and vegetables, preferably locally and organically grown. You may find that a local organic box scheme operates near you, so that you can get the best seasonal produce delivered. It should be firm and glossy with sun-ripened colour and a fresh scent. Fresh herbs with the distinctive 'Italian' flavour, like oregano and basil, are easy to cultivate in window boxes or the garden and have an infinitely finer flavour than their dried counterparts. Italian cuisine is not a complicated or sophisticated style of cooking, but relies on fresh flavours, so your recipes will benefit immeasurably by starting with the best ingredients you can find.

Salamis, pancetta, air-dried bresaola, and mortadella sausages are some of the most commonly used meats in Italy. Prosciutto is

Below: Conchiglie with scallops is elegant and simple.

Above: Root vegetables such as sweet potato make for a colourful and richly satisfying risotto.

the most prized of all. But perhaps the single most important ingredient in a modern Italian kitchen is olive oil. The fruity flavour of a fine extra virgin olive oil perfumes any dish it is used in. Buy the best olive oil you can afford: one bottle goes a long way and makes a huge difference to any recipe. Balsamic vinegar has also become widely available outside of Italy in recent years. Made by the slow wood-aging process of wine vinegar, the finest varieties are deliciously mellow and fragrant. The taste is quite sweet and concentrated, so only a little is needed.

The best-known types of rice are Arborio, Vialone Nano and Carnaroli. Dried pasta shapes such as spaghetti and fusilli, pickled capers, pine nuts, sun-dried tomatoes in oil, dried chillies, fennel seeds and dried porcini mushrooms (soaked in water) are some of the other ingredients commonly used in Italian dishes and are excellent basics to keep in the store cupboard.

The recipes in this book include well-known classics, contemporary seasonal dishes and family favourites to be enjoyed on all occasions, by people of all ages.

Fresh Egg Pasta

In Italy, there has long been a tradition of making fresh pasta. The choice of flavours and fillings is ever increasing by popular demand. Use pasta flour if you can obtain it, as it is very finely ground. Otherwise, use standard plain flour. If you have a pasta rolling machine, use it instead of a rolling pin for steps 5 and 6.

To Serve 3–4
2 eggs, salt
140g/5oz/1 cup flour

To Serve 4–6
3 eggs, salt
210g/7½oz/1½ cups flour

To Serve 6–8
4 eggs, salt
280g/10oz/2 cups flour

1 Place the flour in the centre of a clean, smooth work surface. Make a well in the middle. Break the eggs into the well. Add a pinch of salt.

2 Start beating the eggs with a fork, gradually drawing the flour from the inside walls of the well. As the paste begins to thicken, continue mixing with your hands. Incorporate as much flour as possible, until the mixture forms a mass. It should still be lumpy at this stage. If the dough still sticks to your hands, add a little more plain flour. Set the dough aside. Scrape off all traces of the dough from the work surface until it is perfectly smooth and clean. Wash and dry your hands.

3 Lightly flour the work surface. Knead the dough by pressing it away from you with the heel of your hands, and then folding it over toward you. Repeat this action over and over, turning the dough as you knead. Work for about 10 minutes, or until the dough is smooth and elastic. Do not skimp on the kneading time or the finished pasta will not be light and silky.

4 If you are using more than 2 eggs, divide the dough in half to make it easier to work with. Flour the rolling pin and the work surface. Pat the dough into a disc and begin rolling it out into a flat circle, rotating it one quarter turn after each roll to keep it round. Continue rolling until the disc is about 3mm/⅛in thick.

5 Roll out the dough until it is paper thin by rolling up on to the rolling pin and simultaneously giving a sideways stretching with the hands. Wrap the near edge of the dough around the centre of the rolling pin, and begin to roll the dough up away from you. As you roll back and forth, slide your hands from the centre towards the outer edges of the pin, carefully stretching and thinning out the pasta.

6 Quickly repeat these movements until about two-thirds of the sheet of pasta is wrapped around the pin. Lift and turn the wrapped pasta sheet diagonally before unrolling it Repeat the rolling and stretching process, starting from a new point on the sheet each time to keep it evenly thin. You should do this for 8–10 minutes until the sheet is smooth and almost transparent all over.

7 Leave the sheet to dry out and rest on a clean dish towel or rack for about 25 minutes. It is then ready to cut to shape.

Rigatoni with Winter Tomato Sauce

In winter, when fresh tomatoes are not at their best, this is the sauce the Italians make. Canned tomatoes combined with soffritto (the sautéed mixture of chopped onion, carrot, celery and garlic) and herbs give a better flavour than winter tomatoes.

Serves 6–8
60ml/4 tbsp olive oil
1 garlic clove, thinly sliced
1 onion, finely chopped
1 carrot, finely chopped
1 celery stick, finely chopped
a few leaves each fresh basil, thyme and oregano or marjoram
2 x 400g/14oz cans chopped Italian plum tomatoes
15ml/1 tbsp sun-dried tomato paste
5ml/1 tsp sugar
about 90ml/6 tbsp dry red or white wine (optional)
350g/12oz/3 cups dried rigatoni
salt and ground black pepper
coarsely shaved Parmesan cheese, to serve
chopped fresh mixed herbs, to garnish (optional)

1 Heat the olive oil in a medium pan, add the garlic slices and stir over very low heat for 1–2 minutes.

2 Add the chopped onion, carrot and celery and the fresh herbs. Cook over a low heat, stirring frequently, for 5–7 minutes, until the vegetables have softened and are lightly coloured.

3 Add the canned tomatoes, tomato paste and sugar, then stir in the wine, if using. Add salt and pepper to taste. Bring to the boil, stirring, then lower the heat to a gentle simmer. Cook, uncovered, for about 45 minutes, stirring occasionally to prevent sticking on the bottom of the pan.

4 Bring a pan of lightly salted water to the boil and cook the pasta until al dente. Drain and turn into a warmed serving bowl.

5 Taste the sauce for seasoning, pour the sauce over the pasta and toss well. Garnish with chopped fresh herbs and serve with shavings of Parmesan handed around separately.

Energy 226Kcal/956kJ; Fat 6.6g; Saturated Fat 1g; Carbohydrate 37.8g; Fibre 2.7g

Spaghetti in Fresh Tomato Sauce

This is the famous Neapolitan sauce that is made in summer when tomatoes are very ripe and sweet. It is very simple, so that nothing detracts from the flavour of the tomatoes themselves. It is served here with spaghetti, which is the traditional choice of pasta.

Serves 4

675g/1½lb ripe Italian plum tomatoes
60ml/4 tbsp olive oil
1 onion, finely chopped
350g/12oz fresh or dried spaghetti
1 small handful fresh basil leaves
salt and ground black pepper
shaved Parmesan cheese, to serve

1 With a sharp knife, cut a cross in the base of each tomato. Bring a medium pan of water to the boil and remove from the heat. Plunge a few of the tomatoes into the water, leave for 30 seconds or so, then lift them out with a slotted spoon. Repeat with the remaining tomatoes, then peel off the skins and roughly chop the flesh.

2 Heat the oil in a large pan, add the chopped onion and cook over low heat, stirring frequently, for about 5 minutes, until softened and lightly coloured. Add the tomatoes, with salt and pepper to taste, bring to a simmer, then turn the heat down to low and cover. Cook, stirring occasionally, for 30–40 minutes, until thick.

3 Meanwhile, bring a pan of lightly salted water to the boil, add the pasta and cook until al dente. Shred the basil leaves finely.

4 Remove the sauce from the heat, stir in the basil and taste for seasoning. Drain the pasta, transfer it to a warmed serving bowl, pour the sauce over and toss well. Serve immediately, with coarsely shaved Parmesan handed separately.

Cook's Tip
The Italian plum tomatoes called San Marzano are the best variety to use. When fully ripe, their thin skins peel off easily.

Energy 431Kcal/1821kJ; Fat 13.2g; Saturated Fat 1.9g; Carbohydrate 70.4g; Fibre 4.9g

Pasta with Uncooked Tomato Sauce

This is a wonderfully simple uncooked tomato sauce that goes well with many different kinds of pasta, both long strands and short shapes. It is always made in summer when plum tomatoes have ripened on the vine in the sun and have their fullest flavour. The ricotta salata gives it extra texture and flavour.

Serves 4

500g/1¼lb ripe Italian plum tomatoes
1 large handful fresh basil leaves
75ml/5 tbsp extra virgin olive oil
115g/4oz ricotta salata cheese, diced
1 garlic clove, crushed
350g/12oz/3 cups dried pasta
salt and ground black pepper
coarsely shaved Pecorino cheese, to serve

1 Roughly chop the plum tomatoes, removing the cores and as many of the seeds as you can. Tear the basil leaves into shreds with your fingers.

2 Put the tomatoes in a bowl with the basil, olive oil, diced ricotta and garlic. Add salt and pepper to taste and stir well. Cover and leave at room temperature for 1–2 hours to allow the flavours to mingle.

3 Meanwhile, bring a pan of lightly salted water to the boil, add the pasta and cook until al dente.

4 Drain the pasta and transfer to a large serving dish. Taste the tomato sauce to check the seasoning, then pour it over the hot pasta. Serve immediately with shavings of Pecorino handed around separately in a small bowl.

Cook's Tip
Ricotta salata is a salted and dried version of ricotta cheese. It is firmer than the traditional soft white ricotta, and can be easily diced, crumbled and even grated. It is available from specialist delicatessens. If you have a problem finding it, try using feta cheese instead.

Energy 196Kcal/813kJ; Fat 18.3g; Saturated Fat 4.7g; Carbohydrate 4.8g; Fibre 1.3g

Tagliatelle with Sun-dried Tomatoes

Sun-dried tomatoes, with their intense flavour, are combined with fresh plum tomatoes to make a tasty sauce that is perfect with any type of pasta.

Serves 4

1 garlic clove, crushed
1 celery stick, finely sliced
115g/4oz/1 cup sun-dried
    tomatoes, finely chopped
90ml/3½fl oz/scant ½ cup
    red wine
8 plum tomatoes
350g/12oz dried tagliatelle
salt and ground black pepper

1 Put the garlic, celery, sun-dried tomatoes and wine into a large pan. Gently cook for about 15 minutes.

2 Slash the bottoms of the plum tomatoes and plunge into a pan of boiling water for 1 minute, then transfer them to a pan of cold water. Slip off their skins. Cut in half, remove the seeds and cores and roughly chop the flesh.

3 Add the plum tomatoes to the pan and simmer for a further 5 minutes. Season to taste.

4 Meanwhile, bring a pan of lightly salted water to the boil, add the pasta and cook until al dente. Drain well. Toss with half the sauce and serve on warmed plates, with the remaining sauce spooned over each serving.

Cook's Tip

Sun-drying tomatoes intensifies their flavour and is a way of savouring the full taste of tomatoes in winter. In Italy, it is still possible to find tomatoes that have been literally dried in the sun, but the commercially produced "sun-dried" varieties are usually air-dried by machine. A wrinkled, dark red colour, they are sold dry in packets or preserved in olive oil. Both types are suitable for this recipe. Usually it is best to soak the dry type in hot water until soft before using in a recipe.

Fusilli with Peppers & Onions

Peppers are characteristic of southern Italy. When grilled and peeled they have a delicious smoky flavour, and are easier to digest. Simply team them up with red onion and garlic that has been lightly cooked in olive oil, to make an easy pasta sauce bursting with authentic Italian flavours.

Serves 4

450g/1lb red and yellow
    (bell) peppers
90ml/6 tbsp olive oil
1 large red onion, thinly sliced
2 garlic cloves, minced
400g/14oz/3½ cups fusilli
45ml/3 tbsp finely chopped
    fresh parsley
salt and ground black pepper
freshly grated Parmesan cheese,
    to serve

1 Place the peppers under a hot grill (broiler) and turn occasionally until they are black and blistered on all sides. Remove from the heat, place in a plastic bag and leave for 5 minutes.

2 Peel the skin from the peppers. Cut them into quarters, remove the cores and seeds and slice into thin strips.

3 Heat the oil in a large frying pan. Add the onion and cook over medium heat for 5–8 minutes, until it is translucent. Stir in the garlic and cook for a further 2 minutes.

4 Bring a pan of lightly salted water to the boil, add the pasta and cook until al dente.

5 Meanwhile, add the pepper strips to the onion and mix together gently. Stir in about 45ml/3 tbsp of the pasta cooking water. Season with salt and pepper to taste, then stir in the chopped parsley.

6 Drain the pasta thoroughly. Add the pasta to the frying pan containing the vegetables and cook over medium heat for 1–2 minutes, stirring constantly to coat the pasta with the vegetable sauce. Serve with the freshly grated Parmesan handed around separately.

Energy 369Kcal/1570kJ; Fat 2.3g; Saturated Fat 0.4g; Carbohydrate 74.9g; Fibre 5.3g

Energy 536kcal/2255kJ; Fat 18.9g; Saturated Fat 2.7g; Carbohydrate 82.8g,; Fibre 5.5g

Linguine with Sun-dried Tomato Pesto

Tomato pesto was once a rarity, but is becoming increasingly popular. It is made using sun-dried tomatoes instead of basil.

Serves 4

25g/1oz/⅓ cup pine nuts
25g/1oz/⅓ cup freshly grated
   Parmesan cheese
50g/2oz/½ cup sun-dried
   tomatoes in olive oil
1 garlic clove, roughly chopped
60ml/4 tbsp olive oil
350g/12oz fresh or dried linguine
ground black pepper
basil leaves, to garnish
coarsely shaved Parmesan cheese,
   to serve

1 Put the pine nuts in a small non-stick frying pan and toss over low to medium heat for 1–2 minutes, or until the nuts are lightly toasted and golden.

2 Turn the nuts into a food processor. Add the Parmesan, sun-dried tomatoes and garlic, with pepper to taste. Process until finely chopped.

3 Gradually add the olive oil to the mixture in the food processor through the feeder tube, with the machine running, until it has all been incorporated evenly and all the ingredients have formed a smooth-looking paste.

4 Bring a pan of lightly salted water to the boil and cook the pasta until al dente. Reserve a little of the cooking water, then drain the pasta. Transfer the pasta to a warmed bowl, add the pesto and a few spoonfuls of the hot water and toss well. Serve garnished with basil leaves. Serve Parmesan separately.

> **Cook's Tip**
> *You can make this pesto up to 2 days in advance and keep it in the refrigerator until ready to use. Place in a bowl, pour a thin film of olive oil over the pesto, then cover the bowl tightly.*

Energy 498Kcal/2096kJ; Fat 21.7g; Saturated Fat 3.7g; Carbohydrate 65.9g; Fibre 2.9g

Fusilli with Tomato & Balsamic Vinegar Sauce

This is a modern Cal-Ital recipe (Californian/Italian). The intense, sweet-sour flavour of balsamic vinegar gives a pleasant kick to a sauce made with canned tomatoes.

Serves 6–8

2 x 400g/14oz cans chopped
   Italian plum tomatoes
2 pieces of sun-dried tomato in
   olive oil, drained and sliced
2 garlic cloves, crushed
45ml/3 tbsp olive oil
5ml/1 tsp sugar
350g/12oz/3 cups fresh or
   dried fusilli
45ml/3 tbsp balsamic vinegar
salt and ground black pepper
coarsely shaved Pecorino cheese
   and rocket (arugula) salad,
   to serve

1 Put the canned and sun-dried tomatoes in a medium pan with the garlic, olive oil and sugar. Add salt and pepper to taste. Bring to the boil, stirring. Lower the heat and simmer for about 30 minutes until reduced.

2 Meanwhile, bring a pan of lightly salted water to the boil, add the pasta and cook until al dente.

3 Add the balsamic vinegar to the sauce and stir to mix evenly. Cook for 1–2 minutes, then remove from the heat and taste for seasoning.

4 Drain the pasta and transfer it to a warmed bowl. Pour the sauce over the pasta and toss well. Serve immediately, with rocket salad and shaved Pecorino handed around separately.

> **Cook's Tip**
> *Balsamic vinegar is made in the area around Modena from local trebbiano grapes. The best is aged in a series of barrels, giving it a slightly syrupy texture and a rich, dark colour.*

Energy 210Kcal/891kJ; Fat 5.2g; Saturated Fat 0.8g; Carbohydrate 36.9g; Fibre 2.5g

Cappelletti with Tomatoes & Cream

Tomatoes, cream and fresh basil are a winning combination. In this very quick and easy recipe, the sauce coats little pasta purses filled with soft cheeses to make a substantial dish for vegetarians. If you prefer a lighter dish, you can use the sauce to coat plain, unstuffed pasta. Small shapes such as penne, farfalle or conchiglie are best.

Serves 4

400ml/14fl oz/1²⁄₃ cups passata
   (bottled, strained tomatoes)
90ml/6 tbsp dry white wine
150ml/¼ pint/²⁄₃ cup double
   (heavy) cream
225g/8oz/2½ cups fresh
   cappelletti
1 small handful fresh basil leaves
60ml/4 tbsp freshly grated
   Parmesan cheese
salt and ground black pepper

1 Pour the passata and wine into a medium pan and stir to mix. Bring to the boil over medium heat, then add the cream and stir until evenly mixed and bubbling. Turn the heat down to low and leave to simmer.

2 Cook the cappelletti until al dente: 5–7 minutes or according to the instructions on the packet. Meanwhile, finely shred most of the basil leaves.

3 Drain the pasta well, return it to the pan and toss it with the grated Parmesan. Taste the sauce for seasoning, pour it over the pasta and toss well. Serve immediately, sprinkled with shredded basil and whole basil leaves.

Cook's Tips
• Cappelletti with a variety of fillings are available at supermarkets and Italian delicatessens. Other stuffed pasta shapes, such as tortelloni and ravioli can be used with this sauce.
• The tomato sauce can be made up to a day ahead, then chilled until ready to use. Reheat gently in a heavy pan while the pasta is cooking.

Energy 479Kcal/2004kJ; Fat 26.2g; Saturated Fat 15.7g; Carbohydrate 45.7g; Fibre 2.7g

Trenette with Pesto, French Beans & Potatoes

In Liguria, it is traditional to serve pesto with trenette, French beans and diced potatoes. The ingredients for making fresh pesto are quite expensive, so the French beans and potatoes are added to help make the pesto go further.

Serves 4
about 40 fresh basil leaves
2 garlic cloves, thinly sliced

25ml/1½ tbsp pine nuts
45ml/3 tbsp freshly grated
   Parmesan cheese, plus extra
   to serve
30ml/2 tbsp freshly grated
   Pecorino cheese, plus extra
   to serve
60ml/4 tbsp extra virgin olive oil
2 potatoes, total weight about
   250g/9oz
100g/3½oz French beans
350g/12oz dried trenette
salt and ground black pepper

1 Put the basil leaves, garlic, pine nuts and cheeses in a blender or food processor and process for about 5 seconds. Add half the olive oil and a pinch of salt and process for 5 seconds more. Stop the machine, remove the lid and scrape down the side of the bowl. Add the remaining olive oil and process for 5–10 seconds.

2 Cut the potatoes in half lengthways. Slice each half crossways into 5mm/¼in thick slices. Top and tail the beans, then cut them into 2cm/¾in pieces. Plunge the potatoes and beans into a large saucepan of salted boiling water and boil, uncovered, for 5 minutes.

3 Add the pasta, bring the water back to the boil, stir well, then cook for 5–7 minutes, or until the pasta is al dente.

4 Meanwhile, put the pesto in a large bowl and add 45–60ml/ 3–4 tbsp of the water used for cooking the pasta. Mix well.

5 Drain the pasta and vegetables, add them to the pesto and toss well. Serve immediately on warmed plates, with extra grated Parmesan and Pecorino handed around separately.

Energy 579Kcal/2436kJ; Fat 23.4g; Saturated Fat 6g; Carbohydrate 76.2g; Fibre 4.3g

Spaghetti with Tomatoes & Herbs

This sauce comes from Spoleto in Umbria. It is a fresh, light sauce in which the tomatoes are cooked for a short time, so it should only be made in summer when tomatoes have a good flavour.

Serves 4
350g/12oz ripe Italian plum tomatoes

30ml/2 tbsp olive oil
1 onion, finely chopped
350g/12oz/3 cups fresh or dried spaghetti
2–3 fresh marjoram sprigs, leaves stripped
salt and ground black pepper
shredded fresh basil, to garnish
freshly grated Pecorino cheese, to serve

1 With a sharp knife, cut a cross in the bottom end of each plum tomato. Bring a medium pan of water to the boil and remove from the heat. Plunge a few of the tomatoes into the water, leave for 30 seconds or so, then lift them out with a slotted spoon and set aside. Repeat with the remaining tomatoes, then peel off the skin when cool and finely chop the flesh.

2 Put the chopped onion in a medium pan with the oil. Stir over low heat. Cook gently for about 10 minutes, stirring frequently, until the onion has softened.

3 Add the tomatoes, with salt and pepper to taste. Stir well and cook, uncovered, for about 10 minutes. Meanwhile, cook the pasta in a pan of lightly salted water until al dente.

4 Remove the sauce from the heat, stir in the marjoram sprigs and taste for seasoning. Drain the pasta and transfer to a warmed bowl. Pour the sauce over the pasta and toss well.

5 Divide among four warmed bowls and serve immediately, sprinkled with shredded basil. Hand the grated Pecorino around separately.

Energy 369Kcal/1564kJ; Fat 7.4g; Saturated Fat 1.1g; Carbohydrate 68.7g; Fibre 3.6g

Paglia e Fieno with Sun-dried Tomatoes & Radicchio

This is a light, modern pasta dish of the kind served in fashionable restaurants. It is the presentation that sets it apart, not the preparation, which is actually very quick and easy.

Serves 4
45ml/3 tbsp pine nuts
350g/12oz dried paglia e fieno

45ml/3 tbsp extra virgin olive oil
30ml/2 tbsp sun-dried tomato paste
2 pieces sun-dried tomatoes in olive oil, drained and cut into very thin slivers
40g/1½oz radicchio leaves, finely shredded
4–6 spring onions (scallions), thinly sliced into rings
salt and ground black pepper

1 Put the pine nuts in a non-stick frying pan and toss over low to medium heat for 1–2 minutes, or until they are lightly toasted and golden. Remove and set aside.

2 Cook the pasta according to the packet instructions, keeping the colours separate by using two pans.

3 While the pasta is cooking, heat 15ml/1 tbsp of the oil in a medium skillet or saucepan. Add the sun-dried tomato paste and the sun-dried tomatoes, then stir in 2 ladlefuls of the water used for cooking the pasta. Simmer until the sauce is slightly reduced, stirring constantly.

4 Mix in the radicchio, then taste and season if necessary. Keep on low heat. Drain the paglia e fieno, keeping the colours separate, and return the noodles to the pans in which they were cooked. Add about 15ml/1 tbsp oil to each pan and toss over medium to high heat, until the pasta is glistening.

5 Arrange a portion of green and white pasta in each of four warmed bowls, then spoon the sun-dried tomato and radicchio mixture in the centre. Sprinkle the spring onions and pine nuts over the top and serve immediately. Before eating, each diner should toss the sauce ingredients with the pasta to mix well.

Energy 474Kcal/1995kJ; Fat 17.7g; Saturated Fat 1.9g; Carbohydrate 69.3g; Fibre 3.7g

Fusilli with Spring Vegetables

In spring, the Italian markets are overflowing with an astonishing range of seasonal vegetables, all bursting with flavour. Local cooks take great delight in turning this abundant produce into fresh-tasting sauces for pasta.

Serves 6
1 or 2 small young carrots
2 spring onions (scallions)
175g/6oz courgettes (zucchini)
2 tomatoes
75g/3oz green beans
1 yellow (bell) pepper
60ml/4 tbsp olive oil
25g/1oz/2 tbsp butter
75g/3oz/³⁄₄ cup shelled peas,
    fresh or frozen
1 garlic clove, finely chopped
5–6 leaves fresh basil, torn
    into pieces
salt and ground black pepper
500g/1¼lb/5 cups short coloured
    or plain pasta such as fusilli,
    penne or farfalle
freshly grated Parmesan cheese,
    to serve

1 Cut the carrots, spring onions, courgettes, tomatoes and beans into small, bite size pieces. Cut the pepper in half, remove the core and seeds, then cut into similar size pieces.

2 Heat the oil and butter in a large frying pan. Add the chopped vegetables and peas and cook over medium heat for 5–6 minutes, stirring occasionally.

3 Add the garlic and the basil to the vegetables in the pan and season with salt and pepper. Cover the pan and cook for 5–8 minutes more, or until the vegetables are just tender.

4 Meanwhile, bring a pan of lightly salted water to the boil. Add the pasta and cook until al dente. Reserve a cupful of the cooking water, then drain the pasta.

5 Transfer the pasta into the pan of sauce and mix well to distribute the vegetables evenly. If the sauce seems too dry, add a few tablespoons of the reserved pasta water.

6 Transfer to a warmed serving dish and serve with the Parmesan handed around separately.

Energy 429Kcal/1810kJ; Fat 13.6g; Saturated Fat 4g; Carbohydrate 68.7g; Fibre 4.9g

Fusilli with Mascarpone & Spinach

This creamy, green sauce tossed in lightly cooked pasta is best served with plenty of sun-dried tomato ciabatta bread and sprigs of fresh thyme.

Serves 4
350g/12oz/3 cups fresh or
    dried fusilli
50g/2oz/¼ cup butter
1 onion, chopped
1 garlic clove, chopped
30ml/2 tbsp fresh thyme leaves
225g/8oz frozen spinach leaves,
    thawed
225g/8oz/1 cup
    mascarpone cheese
salt and ground black pepper
fresh thyme sprigs, to garnish

1 Cook the pasta in plenty of boiling salted water according to the instructions on the packet.

2 Melt the butter in a large pan and fry the onion for 10 minutes, until softened.

3 Stir in the garlic, thyme leaves, spinach and seasoning and heat gently for about 5 minutes, stirring occasionally, until completely heated through.

4 Stir in the mascarpone cheese and cook gently, until heated through. Do not boil.

5 Drain the pasta thoroughly and stir into the sauce. Toss until well coated. Serve immediately, garnished with thyme sprigs.

> **Cook's Tip**
> Mascarpone is a rich Italian cream cheese. If you cannot find any, use ordinary full-fat cream cheese instead.

> **Variation**
> Add one or two spoonfuls of pesto sauce and/or pine nuts into the sauce just before draining the pasta to enhance the herby flavour.

Energy 513kcal/2155kJ; Fat 20.5g; Saturated Fat 11.9g; Carbohydrate 68.8g; Fibre 3.9g

Orecchiette with Broccoli

Puglia, in southern Italy, specializes in imaginative pasta and vegetable combinations. Here the famous ear-shaped pasta from the region is tossed with fresh-tasting broccoli florets and a tangy garlic dressing.

Serves 6
800g/1³⁄₄lb broccoli
450g/1lb/4 cups orecchiette
  or penne
90ml/6 tbsp olive oil
3 garlic cloves, finely chopped
salt and ground black pepper

1 Using a small sharp knife, peel the stems of the broccoli, starting from the base and pulling up towards the florets. Discard the woody parts of the stem. Cut the florets and stems into 5cm/2in pieces.

2 Bring a large pan of water to the boil. Drop in the broccoli, and boil for about 5–8 minutes, until barely tender. Using a slotted spoon, transfer the broccoli pieces from the pan to a serving bowl. Do not discard the cooking water.

3 Add salt to the broccoli cooking water. Bring it back to the boil. Drop in the pasta, stir well and cook until al dente.

4 Meanwhile, heat the oil in a small pan. Add the garlic and cook for 2–3 minutes. Using a fork, mash the garlic to a paste. Cook gently for a further 3–4 minutes.

5 Before draining the pasta, ladle 1–2 cupfuls of the cooking water over the broccoli. Add the drained pasta and the hot oil mixture. Toss well and season with salt and pepper, if necessary. Serve immediately.

Cook's Tip
The pasta is cooked in the broccoli cooking water to help it absorb more of the vegetable's flavour and to keep the nutrients in the dish.

Energy 401Kcal/1688kJ; Fat 13.6g; Saturated Fat 2g; Carbohydrate 58.5g; Fibre 5.1g

Pennoni Rigati with Cauliflower

This is an Italian pasta version of cauliflower cheese. Serve with a fresh green salad for a well-balanced main course dish.

Serves 6
1 cauliflower
475ml/16fl oz/2 cups milk
1 bay leaf
50g/2oz/¹⁄₄ cup butter
50g/2oz/¹⁄₂ cup flour
75g/3oz/³⁄₄ cup freshly grated
  Parmesan or Romano cheese
500g/1¹⁄₄lb/5 cups pennoni rigati,
  tortiglioni, or other short pasta
salt and ground black pepper

1 Bring a large pan of water to the boil. Wash the cauliflower well and divide into florets. Boil the florets for 8–10 minutes until they are just tender. Remove them from the pan with a slotted spoon. Chop the cauliflower into bite size pieces and set aside. Do not discard the cooking water.

2 Make a béchamel sauce by gently heating the milk with the bay leaf in a small pan, without allowing it to boil. Melt the butter in a heavy pan. Add the flour and mix to a paste with a wire whisk, making sure that there are no lumps. Cook gently for 2–3 minutes, whisking constantly: do not allow the mixture to turn brown.

3 Strain the hot milk into the flour and butter mixture and mix with the whisk until smooth.

4 Bring the sauce to the boil, stirring constantly, and cook for 4–5 minutes more. Season with salt and pepper. Add the cheese and stir over low heat until it melts. Stir in the cauliflower pieces.

5 Bring the cauliflower cooking water back to the boil. Add salt, stir in the pasta and cook until al dente. Drain the pasta and transfer to a warm serving bowl.

6 Pour the cauliflower sauce over the pasta. Stir gently together and serve immediately.

Energy 533Kcal/2259kJ; Fat 9.4g; Saturated Fat 4.5g; Carbohydrate 92.7g; Fibre 4.9g

Alfredo's Fettuccine

This simple recipe was invented by a Roman restaurateur called Alfredo, who became famous for serving it with a gold fork and spoon. It tastes wonderful, regardless of how it is served!

Serves 4
50g/2oz/¼ cup butter
200ml/7fl oz/scant 1 cup panna da cucina or double (heavy) cream
50g/2oz/⅔ cup freshly grated Parmesan cheese, plus extra to garnish
350g/12oz fresh fettuccine
salt and ground black pepper

1 Melt the butter in a large pan or frying pan. Add the cream and bring it to the boil. Simmer for 5 minutes, stirring, then add the Parmesan, with salt and pepper to taste, and turn off the heat under the pan.

2 Bring a large pan of lightly salted water to the boil. Drop in the pasta all at once and quickly bring back to the boil, stirring occasionally. Cook for 2–3 minutes until the pasta is al dente. Drain thoroughly.

3 Turn the heat under the pan of cream to low, add the pasta all at once and toss until it is coated in the sauce. Taste for seasoning. Serve immediately, with extra grated Parmesan handed around separately.

Cook's Tips
• *With so few ingredients, it is particularly important to use only the best-quality ones for this dish to be a success. Use good unsalted butter and top-quality Parmesan cheese. The best is Parmigiano-Reggiano – available from Italian delicatessens – which has its name stamped on the rind. Grate it only just before using.*
• *Fresh fettuccine is traditional, so either make it yourself or buy it from an Italian delicatessen. If you cannot get fettuccine, you can use tagliatelle instead.*

Energy 697Kcal/2912kJ; Fat 42.8g; Saturated Fat 26g; Carbohydrate 65.8g; Fibre 2.6g

Vermicelli with Lemon

Fresh and tangy, this makes an excellent first course for a dinner party. It doesn't rely on fresh seasonal ingredients, so it is good at any time of year.

50g/2oz/¼ cup butter
200ml/7fl oz/scant 1 cup panna da cucina or double (heavy) cream
115g/4oz/1¼ cups freshly grated Parmesan cheese
salt and ground black pepper

Serves 4
350g/12oz dried vermicelli
juice of 2 large lemons

1 Bring a pan of lightly salted water to the boil, add the pasta and cook until al dente.

2 Meanwhile, pour the lemon juice into a medium pan. Stir in the butter and cream, then add salt and pepper to taste.

3 Bring to the boil, then lower the heat and simmer for about 4 minutes, stirring occasionally, until the cream reduces slightly.

4 Drain the pasta and return it to the pan it was cooked in. Add the grated Parmesan, then taste the sauce for seasoning and pour it over the pasta. Toss quickly over medium heat until the pasta is evenly coated with the sauce, then divide among four warmed bowls and serve immediately.

Cook's Tip
Lemons vary in the amount of juice they yield. On average, a large fresh lemon will yield 60–90ml/4–6 tbsp. The lemony flavour of this dish is supposed to be quite sharp – but you can use less juice if you prefer.

Variation
For an even tangier taste, add a little grated lemon rind to the sauce when you add the butter and the cream in Step 2.

Energy 706Kcal/2934kJ; Fat 37.9g; Saturated Fat 24.6g; Carbohydrate 70.4g; Fibre 0.1g

Pasta with Roast Tomatoes & Goat's Cheese

Roasting tomatoes brings out their flavour and sweetness, which contrasts perfectly with the sharp taste and creamy texture of goat's cheese. Serve with a crisp green salad flavoured with herbs.

Serves 4
8 large ripe tomatoes
60ml/4 tbsp garlic-infused olive oil
450g/1lb any dried
   pasta shapes
200g/7oz firm goat's
   cheese, crumbled
salt and ground black pepper

1 Preheat the oven to 190°C/375°F/Gas 5. Place the tomatoes in a roasting pan and drizzle over 30ml/2 tbsp of the oil. Season well with salt and pepper and roast for 20–25 minutes, or until soft and slightly charred.

2 Meanwhile, cook the pasta in plenty of salted, boiling water, according to the instructions on the packet. Drain well and return to the pan.

3 Roughly mash the tomatoes with a fork, and stir the contents of the roasting pan into the pasta. Gently stir in the goat's cheese and the remaining oil and serve.

Cook's Tips
• Goat's cheese is not a traditional Italian ingredient but some contemporary recipes use this particular type of cheese. Good ones to try are Chèvre Log or Bucheron from France, but available throughout Europe; Crottin de Chavignol (AOC) and Selles-sur-Cher (AOC), both from the Loire region in France, which are traditional, farmhouse creamery, unpasteurized, natural-rind cheeses.
• Irish goat's cheese is superb. Try Blue Rathgore, Boilie, Corleggy, Croghan, Mine-Gabhar, Oisin (Ireland's only blue goat's milk cheese) or St Tola (made with organic milk, and very popular).

Energy 749Kcal/3156kJ; Fat 31g; Saturated Fat 13g; Carbohydrate 95g; Fibre 6.5g

Fusilli with Wild Mushrooms

A very rich dish with an earthy flavour and lots of garlic, this makes an ideal main course for vegetarians, especially if accompanied by a crisp green salad.

Serves 4
150g/5oz bottled wild mushrooms
   in olive oil
25g/1oz/2 tbsp butter
225g/8oz/2 cups fresh wild
   mushrooms, thinly sliced
5ml/1 tsp finely chopped fresh
   thyme
5ml/1 tsp finely chopped fresh
   marjoram or oregano, plus
   extra to garnish
4 garlic cloves, crushed
350g/12oz/3 cups fresh or
   dried fusilli
200ml/7fl oz/scant 1 cup
   panna da cucina or double
   (heavy) cream
salt and ground black pepper

1 Drain about 15ml/1 tbsp of the oil from the mushrooms into a medium pan. Slice or chop the bottled mushrooms into bite-size pieces, if they are large.

2 Add the butter to the oil in the pan and place over low heat until sizzling. Add the bottled and the fresh mushrooms. Stir in the chopped fresh herbs and the garlic, then add salt and pepper to taste.

3 Simmer the mushrooms over medium heat, stirring frequently, for about 10 minutes or until the fresh mushrooms are soft and tender.

4 Meanwhile, bring a pan of lightly salted water to the boil, add the pasta and cook until al dente.

5 As soon as the mushrooms are cooked, increase the heat to high and toss the mixture with a wooden spoon to drive off any excess liquid. Pour in the cream and bring to the boil, stirring, then taste and add more salt and pepper if needed.

6 Drain the pasta and transfer it to a warmed serving bowl. Pour the sauce over the pasta and toss well. Serve immediately, sprinkled with finely chopped fresh herbs.

Energy 656Kcal/2741kJ; Fat 39.5g; Saturated Fat 21g; Carbohydrate 66.1g; Fibre 3.6g

Garganelli with Asparagus & Cream

A lovely recipe for late spring when bunches of fresh young asparagus are found on sale in shops and markets everywhere.

Serves 4
1 bunch fresh young asparagus, weighing 250–300g/9–11oz
350g/12oz/3 cups dried garganelli
25g/1oz/2 tbsp butter
200ml/7fl oz/scant 1 cup panna da cucina or double (heavy) cream
30ml/2 tbsp dry white wine
90–115g/3½–4oz/1–1¼ cups freshly grated Parmesan cheese
30ml/2 tbsp chopped fresh mixed herbs, such as basil, flat leaf parsley, chervil, marjoram and oregano
salt and ground black pepper

1 Trim off and throw away the woody ends of the asparagus – after trimming, you should have about 200g/7oz asparagus spears. Cut the spears diagonally into pieces that are roughly the same length and shape as the garganelli.

2 Blanch the asparagus stems in salted boiling water for 2 minutes, the tips for 1 minute. Immediately after blanching, drain the asparagus stems and tips, rinse in cold water and set aside.

3 Bring a pan of lightly salted water to the boil and cook the pasta until al dente. Meanwhile, put the butter and cream in a medium pan, add salt and pepper to taste and bring to the boil. Simmer for a few minutes until the cream reduces and thickens, then add the asparagus, wine and about half the grated Parmesan. Taste for seasoning and keep on low heat.

4 Drain the pasta when cooked and transfer to a warm bowl. Pour the sauce over the pasta, sprinkle with the fresh herbs and toss well. Serve topped with the remaining Parmesan.

> **Cook's Tip**
> Garganelli all'uovo (with egg) are just perfect for this dish. You can buy packets of this pasta in Italian delicatessens. Penne (quills) or penne rigate (ridged quills) can also be used.

Energy 716Kcal/2994kJ; Fat 41.3g; Saturated Fat 24.8g; Carbohydrate 67g; Fibre 3.6g

Penne with Artichokes

Artichokes are very popular in Italy, and are often used in sauces for pasta. This sauce is garlicky and rich, the perfect dinner party first course during the globe artichoke season.

Serves 6
juice of ½–1 lemon
2 globe artichokes
30ml/2 tbsp olive oil
1 small fennel bulb, thinly sliced, with feathery tops reserved
1 onion, finely chopped
4 garlic cloves, finely chopped
1 handful fresh flat leaf parsley, roughly chopped
400g/14oz can chopped Italian plum tomatoes
150ml/¼ pint/⅔ cup dry white wine
350g/12oz/3 cups dried penne
10ml/2 tsp capers, chopped
salt and ground black pepper
freshly grated Parmesan cheese, to serve

1 Have ready a bowl of cold water to which you have added the juice of half a lemon. Cut off the artichoke stalks, then discard the outer leaves until the pale inner leaves that are almost white at the base remain.

2 Cut off the tops of these leaves so that the base remains. Cut the base in half lengthways, then prise the hairy "choke" out of the centre with the tip of the knife and discard. Cut the artichokes lengthways into 5mm/¼in slices, adding them immediately to the bowl of acidulated water.

3 Bring a large pan of water to the boil. Add a good pinch of salt, then drain the artichokes and add them immediately to the water. Boil for 5 minutes, drain and set aside.

4 Heat the oil in a large skillet or pan and add the fennel, onion, garlic and parsley. Cook over low to medium heat, stirring frequently, for about 10 minutes, until the fennel has softened and is lightly coloured.

5 Add the tomatoes and wine, with salt and pepper to taste. Bring to the boil, stirring, then lower the heat, cover the pan and simmer for 10–15 minutes. Stir in the artichokes, replace the lid and simmer for 10 minutes more. Meanwhile, cook the pasta in salted boiling water according to the instructions on the packet.

6 Drain the pasta, reserving a little of the cooking water. Stir the capers into the sauce, then taste for seasoning and add the remaining lemon juice if you like.

7 Transfer the pasta into a warmed large bowl, pour the sauce over and toss well to mix, adding a little of the reserved cooking water if you like a runnier sauce. Serve immediately, garnished with the reserved fennel fronds. Hand around a bowl of grated Parmesan separately.

> **Cook's Tip**
> When in season, use fresh Italian plum tomatoes instead of canned tomatoes, for a really flavourful dish.

Energy 268Kcal/1133kJ; Fat 5g; Saturated Fat 0.7g; Carbohydrate 46.7g; Fibre 3.2g

Farfalle with Gorgonzola Cream

Sweet and simple, this sauce has a nutty tang from the blue cheese. It is also good with long pasta, such as spaghetti or trenette.

Serves 4
350g/12oz/3 cups dried farfalle
175g/6oz Gorgonzola cheese, any rind removed, diced

150ml/¼ pint/⅔ cup panna da cucina or double (heavy) cream
pinch of sugar
10ml/2 tsp finely chopped fresh sage, plus fresh sage leaves, to garnish
salt and ground black pepper

1 Bring a large pan of lightly salted water to the boil, add the pasta and cook until al dente.

2 Meanwhile, put the Gorgonzola and cream in a medium pan. Add the sugar and plenty of ground black pepper and heat gently, stirring frequently, until the cheese has melted. Remove the pan from the heat.

3 Drain the cooked pasta well and return it to the pan in which it was cooked. Pour the Gorgonzola sauce into the pan with the drained pasta.

4 Add the chopped sage to the pasta and toss over a medium heat until the pasta is evenly coated. Taste for seasoning, adding salt if necessary, then divide among four warmed bowls. Garnish each portion with sage and serve immediately.

> **Cook's Tip**
> Gorgonzola, Italy's famous blue-veined cheese, is made from the curds of stracchino cheese. The curds are layered to encourage the mould to grow. Originally Gorgonzola was made only in the town of that name, but nowadays it is made all over Lombardy. Its flavour can range from very mild (dolce) to extremely powerful (piccante). The cheeses are matured for 3–5 months.

Energy 639Kcal/2677kJ; Fat 34.4g; Saturated Fat 21.1g; Carbohydrate 66.5g; Fibre 2.6g

Farfalle with Mushrooms & Cheese

Fresh wild mushrooms are very good in this sauce, but they are expensive. To cut the cost, use half wild and half cultivated, or as many wild as you can afford – even a small handful will intensify the mushroom flavour of the sauce.

Serves 4
15g/½oz/¼ cup dried porcini mushrooms
250ml/8fl oz/1 cup warm water
25g/1oz/2 tbsp butter
1 small onion, finely chopped

1 garlic clove, crushed
225g/8oz/3 cups fresh mushrooms, thinly sliced
a few fresh sage leaves, very finely chopped, plus a few whole leaves to garnish
150ml/¼ pint/⅔ cup dry white wine
225g/8oz/2 cups dried farfalle
115g/4oz/½ cup mascarpone cheese
115g/4oz Gorgonzola or torta di Gorgonzola cheese, crumbled
salt and ground black pepper

1 Put the dried porcini in a small bowl with the warm water and soak for 20–30 minutes. Remove the porcini with a slotted spoon and squeeze over the bowl to extract as much liquid as possible. Strain the liquid and set aside. Finely chop the porcini.

2 Melt the butter in a large pan, add the onion and porcini and cook gently, stirring for about 3 minutes, until the onion is soft. Add the garlic and fresh mushrooms, sage, salt and plenty of black pepper. Cook over medium heat, stirring frequently, for about 5 minutes, or until the mushrooms are soft and juicy. Stir in the soaking liquid and the wine and simmer gently.

3 Bring a pan of lightly salted water to the boil and cook the pasta for about 10 minutes, or until al dente.

4 Meanwhile, stir the mascarpone and Gorgonzola into the mushroom sauce. Heat through, stirring, until melted. Taste for seasoning and adjust if necessary.

5 Drain the pasta, add to the sauce and toss to mix. Serve, sprinkled with black pepper and garnished with sage leaves.

Energy 375Kcal/1575kJ; Fat 14.8g; Saturated Fat 8.9g; Carbohydrate 43.4g; Fibre 2.5g

Farfalle with Prawns & Peas

A small amount of saffron in the sauce gives this dish a lovely golden colour.

Serves 4

45ml/3 tbsp olive oil
25g/1oz/2 tbsp butter
2 spring onions
  (scallions), chopped
225g/8oz/1 cup frozen petits pois
  or peas, thawed
400g/14oz/3½ cups farfalle
350g/12oz peeled
  prawns (shrimp)
250ml/8fl oz/1 cup dry white
  wine
a few whole strands saffron or
  1ml/⅛ tsp powdered saffron
salt and ground black pepper
30ml/2 tbsp chopped fresh fennel
  or dill, to serve

1 Heat the oil and butter in a large frying pan and sauté the spring onions lightly. Add the peas and cook for 2–3 minutes.

2 Bring a pan of lightly salted water to the boil, add the pasta and cook until al dente.

3 Meanwhile, add the prawns, wine and saffron to the pan of peas. Increase the heat and cook until the wine is reduced by about half. Add salt and pepper to taste. Cover the pan and reduce the heat to low.

4 Drain the pasta and add to the pan of sauce. Stir over high heat for 1–2 minutes, coating the pasta with the sauce. Sprinkle with the fresh herbs and serve immediately.

Cook's Tip
The Italian coastal waters boast a wide variety of prawns and shrimp, ranging from the small gamberetti, usually served as part of an antipasto, to the larger gamberi rossi, which turn bright red when cooked, and the even bigger gamberoni, large succulent prawns from the Adriatic which have a superb flavour. In Italy they are usually sold raw. Look for medium prawns for this recipe: choose ones that feel firm and have bright shells and a fresh smell. Pre-cooked prawns could also be used.

Energy 624Kcal/2629kJ; Fat 16.5g; Saturated Fat 4.9g; Carbohydrate 88.1g; Fibre 5.1g

Spaghetti with Mussels

Mussels are popular in all the coastal regions of Italy, and are delicious with pasta. This simple dish is greatly improved by using the freshest mussels available.

Serves 4

1kg/2lb fresh mussels, in
  their shells
75ml/5 tbsp olive oil
3 garlic cloves, finely chopped
60ml/4 tbsp finely chopped
  fresh parsley
60ml/4 tbsp white wine
400g/14oz spaghetti
salt and ground black pepper

1 Scrub the mussels well under cold running water, cutting off the beard with a small sharp knife.

2 Place the mussels with a cupful of water in a large pan over moderate heat. As soon as they open, lift them out one by one. When all the mussels have opened (discard any that do not), strain the liquid in the pan through a layer of kitchen paper and reserve until needed.

3 Bring a pan of lightly salted water to the boil, add the pasta and cook until al dente.

4 Meanwhile, heat the oil in a large frying pan. Add the garlic and parsley and cook for 2–3 minutes. Add the mussels, their strained juices and the wine. Cook over medium heat. Add a generous amount of freshly ground black pepper to the sauce. Taste for seasoning, adding salt as necessary.

5 Drain the pasta and add to the pan of sauce. Stir well over medium heat for 1–2 minutes more. Serve immediately.

Cook's Tip
Mussels should be firmly closed when fresh. If a mussel is slightly open, pinch it closed or tap it on a table. If it remains closed on its own, it is alive. If it remains open, discard it.

Energy 545kcal/2301KJ; Fat 17.2g; Saturated Fat 2.4g; Carbohydrate 74.5g; Fibre 3.5g

Linguine with Scallops & Tomatoes

Garlic-flavoured scallops combine beautifully with tomatoes, pasta and basil to create a simple yet flavourful dish, capturing the very essence of Italian cooking.

Serves 4
450g/1lb fresh or dried linguine
30ml/2 tbsp olive oil
2 garlic cloves, crushed
450g/1lb sea scallops, shelled and
halved horizontally

2.5ml/½ tsp salt
30ml/2 tbsp chopped fresh basil
ground black pepper

For the sauce
30ml/2 tbsp olive oil
½ onion, finely chopped
1 garlic clove, crushed
2 x 400g/14oz cans Italian
plum tomatoes

1 To make the tomato sauce, heat the oil in a non-stick frying pan. Add the onion, garlic and a little salt, and cook over medium heat for about 5 minutes, until just softened, stirring occasionally.

2 Add the tomatoes to the pan, with their juice, and crush with a fork. Bring the mixture to the boil, then reduce the heat and simmer gently for 15 minutes, stirring occasionally. Remove from the heat and set aside.

3 Bring a pan of lightly salted water to the boil, add the pasta and cook until al dente.

4 Meanwhile, heat the oil in another non-stick frying pan and cook the garlic for about 30 seconds, until just sizzling. Add the scallops and the salt and cook over high heat, for about 3 minutes, tossing the pan, until the scallops are cooked through.

5 Add the scallops to the tomato sauce. Season with salt and pepper, stir and keep warm.

6 Drain the pasta, rinse under hot water and drain again. Place in a large serving dish. Add the sauce and the basil and toss together thoroughly. Serve the pasta immediately.

Energy 656Kcal/2777kJ; Fat 15.2g; Saturated Fat 2.5g; Carbohydrate 94.6g; Fibre 5.5g

Linguine with Clam & Tomato Sauce

There are two types of traditional Italian clam sauce for pasta: one with tomatoes and one without. This is the tomato version.

Serves 4
1kg/2lb fresh clams in their shells,
or 350g/12oz canned clams,
with their liquid

90ml/6 tbsp olive oil
1 garlic clove, crushed
400g/14oz tomatoes, fresh or
canned, very finely chopped
400g/14oz linguine
60ml/4 tbsp chopped
fresh parsley
salt and ground black pepper

1 Scrub and rinse the clams well under cold running water. Place them in a large pan with a cupful of water and heat until the clams begin to open. Lift each clam out as soon as it opens and scoop it out of its shell using a small spoon. Place in a bowl.

2 If the clams are large, chop them into 2 or 3 pieces. Reserve any liquids from the shells in a separate bowl. When all the clams have opened (discard any that do not open) pour the cooking liquid into the juices from the clams, then strain through a piece of kitchen paper to remove any sand. If using canned clams, use the liquid from the can and the cooking liquid.

3 Bring a pan of lightly salted water to the boil and cook the pasta until al dente.

4 Meanwhile, place the olive oil in a medium pan with the crushed garlic. Cook over medium heat, until the garlic is just golden. Remove the garlic and discard. Add the chopped tomatoes to the oil and pour in the clam liquid. Mix well and cook until the sauce begins to dry out and thicken slightly.

5 Stir the parsley and the clams into the tomato sauce, and increase the heat. Add salt and pepper to taste. Drain the pasta and transfer it into a serving bowl. Pour on the hot sauce and mix well before serving.

Energy 579Kcal/2441kJ; Fat 19.3g; Saturated Fat 2.8g; Carbohydrate 79.2g; Fibre 4.5g

Macaroni with King Prawns & Ham

Radicchio makes a novel addition to this sauce. The bitter flavour of the leaves mellows on cooking and perfectly complements the richness of the shellfish.

Serves 4
350g/12oz/3 cups dried
   short macaroni
45ml/3 tbsp olive oil
12 raw king prawns (jumbo
   shrimp), peeled
1 garlic clove, chopped
175g/6oz/generous 1 cup diced
   smoked ham
150ml/¼ pint/⅔ cup red wine
½ small radicchio
   lettuce, shredded
2 egg yolks, beaten
30ml/2 tbsp chopped fresh flat
   leaf parsley
150ml/¼ pint/⅔ cup double
   (heavy) cream
salt and ground black pepper
shredded fresh basil, to garnish

1 Bring a pan of lightly salted water to the boil, add the pasta and cook until al dente.

2 Meanwhile, heat the oil in a frying pan and cook the prawns, garlic and ham for about 5 minutes, stirring occasionally, until the prawns are just opaque and tender. Be careful not to overcook the prawns.

3 Add the wine and radicchio, bring to the boil and boil rapidly until the juices are reduced by about half. Remove from the heat, add the egg yolks to the sauce and stir well to blend.

4 Stir in the parsley and cream and bring almost to the boil, stirring constantly, then simmer until the sauce thickens slightly. Check the seasoning and adjust if necessary.

5 Drain the pasta thoroughly and toss in the sauce to coat. Serve immediately, garnished with some shredded fresh basil.

Cook's Tip
To peel prawns, pull off the heads, peel off the body shell and legs, then pick out the black vein running down the back.

Energy 707Kcal/2963kJ; Fat 34.7g; Saturated Fat 15.2g; Carbohydrate 66.7g; Fibre 3.3g

Black Tagliatelle with Scallops

A stunning pasta dish using black tagliatelle with a contrasting white fish sauce.

Serves 4
120ml/4fl oz/½ cup low-fat
   crème fraîche
10ml/2 tsp wholegrain mustard
2 garlic cloves, crushed
30–45ml/2–3 tbsp freshly
   squeezed lime juice
60ml/4 tbsp chopped
   fresh parsley
30ml/2 tbsp snipped chives
350g/12oz fresh or dried black
   tagliatelle
12 large fresh scallops, shelled
60ml/4 tbsp white wine
150ml/¼ pint/⅔ cup fish stock
salt and ground black pepper
lime wedges and parsley sprigs,
   to garnish

1 To make the tartare sauce, mix the crème fraîche, mustard, garlic, lime juice, herbs and seasoning together in a bowl.

2 Bring a pan of lightly salted water to the boil, add the pasta and cook until al dente. Drain the pasta thoroughly.

3 Slice each of the scallops in half horizontally. Keep any coral whole. Put the white wine and fish stock into a medium pan and heat until the mixture reaches simmering point. Add the scallops to the pan and cook very gently for 3–4 minutes (do not be tempted to cook them for any longer or they will become tough).

4 Remove the scallops from the pan with a slotted spoon. Boil the wine and stock to reduce by half and add the tartare sauce to the pan.

5 Heat the combined mixture gently to warm, replace the scallops and cook gently for 1 minute. Spoon over the pasta and garnish with lime wedges and sprigs of parsley.

Cook's Tip
Dramatic-looking black tagliatelle is flavoured and coloured with squid ink. It is suitable for seafood pasta dishes.

Energy 417Kcal/1767kJ; Fat 6.8g; Saturated Fat 3.4g; Carbohydrate 68g; Fibre 2.6g

Fusilli with Vegetable & Prawn Sauce

You will need to start this recipe the day before because the prawns should be left to marinate overnight.

Serves 4

450g/1lb peeled prawns (shrimp)
60ml/4 tbsp soy sauce
45ml/3 tbsp olive oil
350g/12oz/3 cups fusilli col buco
1 yellow (bell) pepper, cored, seeded and cut into strips
225g/8oz broccoli florets
1 bunch spring onions (scallions), shredded
2.5cm/1in piece fresh root ginger, peeled and shredded
15ml/1 tbsp chopped fresh oregano
30ml/2 tbsp dry sherry
15ml/1 tbsp cornflour (cornstarch)
300ml/½ pint/1¼ cups fish stock
salt and ground black pepper

1 Place the prawns in a mixing bowl. Stir in half the soy sauce and 30ml/2 tbsp of the olive oil. Cover and marinate overnight in the refrigerator.

2 Bring a pan of lightly salted water to the boil, add the pasta and cook until al dente.

3 Meanwhile, heat the remaining oil in a wok or frying pan and fry the prawns for 1 minute, stirring.

4 Add the pepper, broccoli, spring onions, ginger and oregano and fry, stirring, for about 1–2 minutes.

5 Drain the pasta thoroughly, set aside and keep warm. Meanwhile, in a bowl, blend together the sherry and cornflour until smooth. Stir in the fish stock and remaining soy sauce until well blended.

6 Pour the stock mixture into the wok or pan, bring to the boil and fry, stirring constantly, for 2 minutes, until the liquid has thickened. Pour the prawn mixture over the pasta, toss lightly together and serve immediately.

Energy 477Kcal/2022kJ; Fat 5.9g; Saturated Fat 0.9g; Carbohydrate 74.3g; Fibre 5.2g

Tagliatelle with Saffron Mussels

Mussels in a delicate saffron and cream sauce are served with tagliatelle in this recipe, but you can use any other type of pasta if you prefer.

Serves 4

1.75kg/4lb fresh mussels, in their shells
2 shallots, chopped
150ml/¼ pint/⅔ cup dry white wine
350g/12oz dried tagliatelle
25g/1oz/2 tbsp butter
2 garlic cloves, crushed
250ml/8fl oz/1 cup double (heavy) cream
generous pinch saffron threads
1 egg yolk
salt and ground black pepper
30ml/2 tbsp chopped fresh parsley, to garnish

1 Scrub the mussels well under cold running water. Remove the beards and discard any mussels that are open.

2 Place the mussels in a large pan with the shallots and pour over the wine. Cover and cook over high heat, shaking the pan occasionally, for 5–8 minutes, until the mussels have opened. Drain the mussels, reserving the liquid. Discard any that remain closed. Shell all but a few of the mussels and keep warm.

3 Bring the reserved cooking liquid to the boil in the pan, then reduce by half. Strain the liquid into a jug to remove any grit.

4 Bring a pan of lightly salted water to the boil, add the tagliatelle and cook until al dente.

5 Meanwhile, melt the butter in a large frying pan and fry the garlic for 1 minute. Pour in the mussel liquid, cream and saffron threads. Heat gently until the sauce thickens slightly.

6 Remove the pan from the heat, stir in the egg yolk and shelled mussels and season the sauce to taste.

7 Drain the tagliatelle and transfer to warmed serving dishes. Spoon the sauce over and sprinkle with chopped parsley. Garnish with the mussels in shells and serve at once.

Energy 815Kcal/3415kJ; Fat 44.3g; Saturated Fat 25.1g; Carbohydrate 67.4g; Fibre 2.8g

Pink & Green Farfalle

In this modern recipe, pink prawns and green courgettes combine prettily with cream and pasta bows to make a substantial main course. Serve with crusty Italian rolls or chunks of warm ciabatta bread.

Serves 4
50g/2oz/¼ cup butter
2–3 spring onions (scallions), very thinly sliced on the diagonal
350g/12oz courgettes (zucchini), thinly sliced on the diagonal
60ml/4 tbsp dry white wine
300g/11oz/2⅔ cups dried farfalle
75ml/5 tbsp crème fraîche
225g/8oz/1⅓ cups peeled cooked prawns (shrimp), thawed and thoroughly dried if frozen
15ml/1 tbsp finely chopped fresh marjoram or flat leaf parsley, or a mixture
salt and ground black pepper

1 Melt the butter in a large pan, add the sliced spring onions and cook over low heat, stirring frequently, for about 5 minutes, until softened. Add the sliced courgettes, with salt and pepper to taste, and cook, stirring frequently, for 5 minutes. Pour over the wine and let it bubble, then cover and simmer for 10 minutes.

2 Bring a pan of lightly salted water to the boil, add the pasta and cook until al dente.

3 Meanwhile, add the crème fraîche to the courgette mixture in the pan and simmer for about 10 minutes until the sauce is well reduced.

4 Add the prawns to the courgette mixture, heat through gently and taste for seasoning. Drain the pasta and transfer it into a warmed bowl. Pour the sauce over, add the chopped herbs and toss well. Serve immediately.

> **Variation**
> Use dried penne instead of the farfalle, and try replacing the courgettes with asparagus tips.

Penne with Prawns & Pernod

This recipe is typical of those found on menus in the most innovative Italian restaurants. You could use white wine and basil instead of Pernod and dill.

Serves 4
200ml/7fl oz/scant 1 cup panna da cucina or double (heavy) cream
250ml/8fl oz/1 cup fish stock
350g/12oz/3 cups dried penne
30–45ml/2–3 tbsp Pernod
225g/8oz/1⅓ cups peeled cooked prawns (shrimp), thawed and thoroughly dried if frozen
30ml/2 tbsp chopped fresh dill, plus extra to garnish
salt and ground black pepper

1 Put the cream and the fish stock in a medium pan and bring to the boil. Lower the heat and simmer, stirring occasionally, for 10–15 minutes, until reduced by about half.

2 Meanwhile, bring a pan of lightly salted water to the boil, add the pasta and cook until al dente.

3 Add the Pernod and prawns to the cream sauce, with salt and pepper to taste, if necessary. Heat the prawns through very gently. Drain the pasta and transfer it to a warmed bowl. Pour the sauce over the pasta, add the dill and toss well. Serve immediately, sprinkled with chopped dill.

Chilli, Anchovy & Tomato Pasta

The sauce for this tasty pasta dish packs a punch, thanks to the robust flavours of red chillies, anchovies and capers.

Serves 4
45ml/3 tbsp olive oil
2 garlic cloves, crushed
2 fresh red chillies, seeded and chopped
6 canned anchovy fillets, drained
500g/1½lb ripe tomatoes, peeled, seeded and chopped
30ml/2 tbsp sun-dried tomato paste
30ml/2 tbsp drained capers
1 cup black pitted olives, roughly chopped
125g/4oz/1 cup dried penne
salt and ground black pepper
roughly chopped fresh basil, to garnish

1 Heat the oil in a large pan, and sauté the garlic and chilli over low heat for 2–3 minutes.

2 Add the anchovies, mashing them with a fork, then stir in the tomatoes, sun-dried tomato paste, capers and olives. Add salt and pepper to taste. Simmer gently, uncovered, for 20 minutes, stirring occasionally.

3 Meanwhile, bring a large pan of lightly salted water to the boil and add the penne. Cook until al dente.

4 Drain the pasta, return it to the clean pan and add the sauce. Mix thoroughly, transfer to a heated serving dish, garnish with the basil and serve immediately.

Energy 490Kcal/2058kJ; Fat 19.8g; Saturated Fat 11.9g; Carbohydrate 57.9g; Fibre 3g

Top Energy 607Kcal/2544kJ; Fat 28.8g; Saturated Fat 16.9g; Carbohydrate 66g; Fibre 2.6g
Above Energy 445Kcal/1850kJ; Fat 34.8g; Saturated Fat 5g; Carbohydrate 28.4g; Fibre 2.9g

Ravioli with Crab

This recipe uses chilli-flavoured pasta, which looks and tastes good with crab, but you can use plain pasta.

Serves 4
1 quantity handmade Egg Pasta (see page 6) flavoured with chillies (optional)
flour, for dusting
90g/3½oz/7 tbsp butter
juice of 1 lemon

For the filling
175g/6oz/¾ cup mascarpone cheese
175g/6oz/¾ cup crabmeat
30ml/2 tbsp finely chopped fresh flat leaf parsley
finely grated rind of 1 lemon
pinch of crushed dried chillies (optional)
salt and ground black pepper

1 To make the filling, put the mascarpone in a bowl and mash it with a fork. Add the crabmeat, parsley, lemon rind, crushed dried chillies (if using) and salt and pepper to taste. Stir well.

2 Using a pasta machine, roll out one-quarter of the pasta into a 90cm–1m/36in–3ft strip. Cut the strip with a sharp knife into two 45–50cm/18–20in lengths (you can do this during rolling if the strip gets too long to manage).

3 With a 6cm/2½in fluted cutter, cut out 8 squares from each pasta strip. Using a teaspoon, put a mound of filling in the centre of half the discs. Brush a little water around the edge of the discs, then top with the plain discs; press the edges to seal. For a decorative finish, press the edges with the tines of a fork.

4 Put the ravioli on floured dish towels, sprinkle lightly with flour and leave to dry while repeating the process with the rest of the dough to make 32 ravioli. If you have any stuffing left, you can re-roll the pasta trimmings and make more ravioli.

5 Cook the ravioli in a large pan of salted boiling water for 4–5 minutes. Meanwhile, melt the butter and lemon juice in a small pan until sizzling. Drain the ravioli and divide equally among four warmed bowls. Drizzle the lemon butter over and serve immediately.

Energy 581Kcal/2437kJ; Fat 26.8g; Saturated Fat 15.9g; Carbohydrate 66.3g; Fibre 2.6g

Penne with Prawns & Artichokes

This is a good dish to make in late spring or early summer, when greeny-purple baby artichokes appear on the scene.

Serves 4
juice of ½ lemon
4 baby artichokes
90ml/6tbsp olive oil

2 garlic cloves, crushed
30ml/2 tbsp chopped fresh mint
30ml/2 tbsp chopped fresh flat leaf parsley
350g/12oz/3 cups dried penne
8–12 peeled, cooked large pawns (shrimp), each cut into 2–3 pieces
25g/1oz/2 tbsp butter
salt and ground black pepper

1 Have ready a bowl of cold water to which you have added the lemon juice. To prepare the artichokes, cut off the artichoke stalks, if any, and cut across the tops of the leaves. Peel off and discard any tough or discoloured outer leaves.

2 Cut the artichokes lengthways into quarters and remove any hairy "chokes" from their centres. Finally, cut the pieces of artichoke lengthways into 5mm/¼in slices and put these in the bowl of acidulated water.

3 Drain the slices of artichoke and pat them dry. Heat the olive oil in a non-stick frying pan and add the artichokes, the crushed garlic and half the mint and parsley to the pan.

4 Season with plenty of salt and pepper. Cook over low heat, stirring frequently, for about 10 minutes, or until the artichokes feel tender when pierced with a sharp knife.

5 Meanwhile, bring a pan of lightly salted water to the boil, add the pasta and cook until al dente.

6 Add the prawns to the artichokes, stir well to mix, then heat through gently for 1–2 minutes.

7 Drain the pasta and turn into a warmed bowl. Add the butter and toss until melted. Spoon the artichokes over the pasta and toss together. Serve sprinkled with the remaining herbs.

Energy 519Kcal/2181kJ; Fat 23.6g; Saturated Fat 5.8g; Carbohydrate 65.5g; Fibre 3.5g

Vermicelli with Clam & Chilli Sauce

This recipe comes from the city of Naples, where both fresh tomato sauce and seafood are traditionally served with vermicelli.

Serves 4

1kg/2¼lb fresh clams
250ml/8fl oz/1 cup dry white wine
2 garlic cloves, bruised
1 large handful fresh flat leaf parsley
30ml/2 tbsp olive oil
1 small onion, finely chopped
8 ripe Italian plum tomatoes, peeled, seeded and finely chopped
½–1 fresh red chilli, seeded and finely chopped
350g/12oz dried vermicelli
salt and ground black pepper

1 Scrub the clams thoroughly under cold running water and discard any that are open or do not close when sharply tapped.

2 Pour the wine into a large pan, add the garlic and half the parsley, then the clams. Cover tightly and bring to the boil over high heat. Cook for 5 minutes, shaking, until the clams open.

3 Transfer the clams to a large colander set over a bowl and let the liquid drain through. When cool enough to handle, remove about two-thirds from their shells, tipping the clam liquid into the bowl of cooking liquid. Discard any unopened clams. Set the clams aside; keep the unshelled clams warm in a covered bowl.

4 Heat the oil in a pan, add the onion and cook gently, stirring, for about 5 minutes, until lightly coloured. Add the tomatoes, then strain in the clam cooking liquid. Add the chilli, then season.

5 Bring to the boil, half cover and simmer gently for 15–20 minutes. Meanwhile, cook the pasta in lightly salted boiling water until al dente. Chop the remaining parsley finely.

6 Add the shelled clams to the tomato sauce, stir well and heat through very gently for 2–3 minutes. Drain the pasta well and transfer it to a warmed bowl. Taste the sauce for seasoning, then pour the sauce over the pasta and toss together well. Garnish with the reserved clams and chopped parsley.

Conchiglie & Scallops

A thoroughly modern dish, this warm salad consists of succulent wine-cooked scallops tossed into pasta with tangy leaves and a chilli-flavoured dressing.

Serves 4

8 large fresh scallops, shelled
300g/11oz/2¾ cups dried conchiglie
15ml/1 tbsp olive oil
15g/½oz/1 tbsp butter
120ml/4fl oz/½ cup dry white wine
90g/3½oz rocket (arugula) leaves, stalks trimmed
salt and ground black pepper

For the vinaigrette

60ml/4 tbsp extra virgin olive oil
15ml/1 tbsp balsamic vinegar
1 piece bottled roasted (bell) pepper, drained and finely chopped
1–2 fresh red chillies, seeded and chopped
1 garlic clove, crushed
5–10ml/1–2 tsp clear honey

1 Cut each scallop into 2–3 pieces. If the corals are attached, pull them off and cut each piece in half. Season the scallops and corals with salt and pepper.

2 To make the vinaigrette, put the oil, vinegar, chopped pepper and chillies in a jug with the garlic and honey and whisk well.

3 Bring a pan of lightly salted water to the boil, add the pasta and cook until al dente.

4 Meanwhile, heat the oil and butter in a non-stick frying pan until sizzling. Add half the scallops and toss over high heat for 2 minutes. Remove with a slotted spoon and keep warm. Cook the remaining scallops in the same way.

5 Add the wine to the liquid remaining in the pan and stir over high heat, until the mixture has reduced to a few tablespoons. Remove from the heat and keep warm.

6 Drain the pasta and transfer it to a warmed bowl. Add the rocket, scallops, the reduced cooking juices and the vinaigrette and toss well to combine. Serve immediately.

Energy 504Kcal/2119kJ; Fat 7g; Saturated Fat 1.1g; Carbohydrate 76.8g; Fibre 2.1g

Energy 504Kcal/2119kJ; Fat 19.1g; Saturated Fat 4.3g; Carbohydrate 60.6g; Fibre 2.9g

Tagliatelle with Scallops

Scallops and brandy make this a relatively expensive dish, but it is so delicious that you will find it well worth the cost. Serve it for a dinner party first course.

Serves 4

200g/7oz fresh scallops, shelled and sliced
30ml/2 tbsp plain (all-purpose) flour
275g/10oz fresh spinach-flavoured tagliatelle
40g/1½oz/3 tbsp butter
2 spring onions (scallions), cut into thin rings
½–1 small fresh red chilli, seeded and very finely chopped
30ml/2 tbsp finely chopped fresh flat leaf parsley
60ml/4 tbsp brandy
105ml/7 tbsp fish stock
salt and ground black pepper

1 Toss the scallops in the flour, then shake off the excess.

2 Bring a pan of lightly salted water to the boil, add the pasta and cook until al dente.

3 Meanwhile, melt the butter in a frying pan or large pan. Add the spring onions, finely chopped chilli and half the parsley and fry, stirring frequently, for 1–2 minutes over medium heat. Add the scallops and toss over the heat for 1–2 minutes.

4 Pour the brandy over the scallops, then set it alight with a match. As soon as the flames have died down, stir in the fish stock and salt and pepper to taste. Mix well. Simmer for 2–3 minutes, then cover the pan and remove it from the heat.

5 Drain the pasta, add to the sauce and toss over medium heat until mixed. Serve at once, in warmed bowls sprinkled with the remaining parsley.

> **Cook's Tip**
> *Buy fresh scallops, with their corals if possible. Fresh scallops always have a better texture and flavour than frozen scallops, which tend to be watery.*

Spaghetti with Squid & Peas

In Tuscany, squid is often cooked with peas in a tomato sauce. This recipe is a variation on the theme, and it works very well.

Serves 4

450g/1lb prepared squid
30ml/2 tbsp olive oil
1 small onion, finely chopped
400g/14oz can chopped Italian plum tomatoes
1 garlic clove, finely chopped
15ml/1 tbsp red wine vinegar
5ml/1 tsp sugar
10ml/2 tsp finely chopped fresh rosemary
115g/4oz/1 cup frozen peas
350g/12oz fresh or dried spaghetti
15ml/1 tbsp chopped fresh flat leaf parsley
salt and ground black pepper

1 Cut the prepared squid into strips about 5mm/¼in wide. Finely chop any tentacles.

2 Heat the oil in a frying pan or medium pan, add the finely chopped onion and cook gently, stirring, for about 5 minutes, until softened. Add the squid, tomatoes, garlic, red wine vinegar and sugar.

3 Add the rosemary, with salt and pepper to taste. Bring to the boil, stirring, then cover and simmer gently for 20 minutes. Uncover the pan, add the peas and cook for 10 minutes.

4 Meanwhile, bring a pan of lightly salted water to the boil, add the pasta and cook until al dente.

5 Drain the pasta thoroughly and transfer it to a warmed serving bowl. Pour the sauce over the pasta, add the parsley, then toss well and serve.

> **Cook's Tip**
> *Prepared squid consists of the body pouch and tentacles – the head and body contents are removed and discarded. You can usually buy squid ready prepared from fish counters.*

Energy 429Kcal/1809kJ; Fat 10.3g; Saturated Fat 5.6g; Carbohydrate 58.7g; Fibre 2.3g

Energy 490Kcal/2076kJ; Fat 9.8g; Saturated Fat 1.6g; Carbohydrate 74.8g; Fibre 5.1g

Spaghetti with Salmon & Prawns

This is a lovely, fresh-tasting pasta dish, perfect for an alfresco meal in summer.

Serves 4
300g/11oz salmon fillet
200ml/7fl oz/scant 1 cup dry white wine
a few fresh basil sprigs, plus extra basil leaves to garnish
6 ripe Italian plum tomatoes, peeled and finely chopped
150ml/1/4 pint/2/3 cup double (heavy) cream
350g/12oz fresh or dried spaghetti
115g/4oz/2/3 cup peeled cooked prawns (shrimp), thawed and thoroughly dried if frozen
salt and ground black pepper

1 Put the salmon skin-side up in a shallow pan. Pour the wine over, then add the basil to the pan and sprinkle the fish with salt and pepper. Bring the wine to the boil, cover the pan and simmer gently for no more than 5 minutes. Using a metal spatula, lift the fish out of the pan and leave to cool a little.

2 Add the tomatoes and cream to the liquid remaining in the pan and bring to the boil. Stir well, then lower the heat and simmer, uncovered, for 10–15 minutes. Meanwhile, cook the pasta in plenty of boiling water until al dente.

3 When cool enough to handle, flake the fish into large chunks, discarding the skin and any bones. Add the fish to the sauce with the prawns, shaking the pan until the fish and shellfish are well coated. Taste for seasoning.

4 Drain the pasta and turn into a warmed bowl. Pour the sauce over the pasta and toss to combine. Serve immediately, garnished with fresh basil leaves.

Cook's Tip
Check the salmon fillet carefully for small bones when you are flaking the flesh. Although the salmon is already filleted, you may find a few stray 'pin' bones. Pick them out carefully using tweezers or your fingertips.

Energy 696Kcal/2923kJ; Fat 30.5g; Saturated Fat 14.3g; Carbohydrate 69.7g; Fibre 3.8g

Tagliolini with Clams & Mussels

Serve on white china to make the most of this colourful dish.

Serves 4
450g/1lb fresh mussels, in their shells
450g/1lb fresh clams, in their shells
60ml/4 tbsp olive oil
1 small onion, finely chopped
2 garlic cloves, finely chopped
1 large handful fresh flat leaf parsley, plus extra to garnish
175ml/6fl oz/3/4 cup dry white wine
250ml/8fl oz/1 cup fish stock
1 small fresh red chilli, seeded and chopped
350g/12oz black tagliolini or tagliatelle
salt and ground black pepper

1 Scrub the mussels and clams under cold running water and discard any that are open or damaged, or that do not close when sharply tapped against the work surface.

2 Heat half the oil in a large pan, add the onion and cook gently for about 5 minutes until softened. Sprinkle in the garlic, then add about half the parsley sprigs and season with salt and pepper to taste.

3 Add the cleaned mussels and clams and pour in the wine. Cover with a lid and bring to the boil over high heat. Cook for about 5 minutes, shaking the pan frequently, until the shellfish have opened.

4 Turn the mussels and clams into a fine sieve (strainer) set over a bowl and let the liquid drain through. Discard the flavourings in the strainer, together with any mussels or clams that have failed to open. Return the liquid to the cleaned out pan and add the fish stock.

5 Chop the remaining parsley finely and add it to the liquid with the chopped chilli. Bring to the boil, then lower the heat and simmer, stirring, for a few minutes, until slightly reduced. Turn off the heat.

6 Remove and discard the top shells from about half the mussels and clams. Put all the mussels and clams in the pan of liquid and seasonings, then cover the pan tightly and set aside.

7 Bring a pan of lightly salted water to the boil, add the pasta and cook until al dente.

8 Drain the pasta well, then return to the clean pan; toss with the remaining olive oil. Put the pan of shellfish over high heat and toss to heat the shellfish through quickly, combine with the liquid and seasonings.

9 Divide the pasta among four warmed plates, spoon the shellfish mixture over, then serve, garnished with parsley.

Variation
If clams are not available, use double the amount of fresh mussels. The chilli can be omitted, if preferred.

Energy 498Kcal/2102kJ; Fat 13.7g; Saturated Fat 2g; Carbohydrate 66.3g; Fibre 3.1g

Linguine with Crab

Serve this glorious dish from Rome with crusty bread, as a foil to the richness.

Serves 4
about 250g/9oz fresh crabmeat
45ml/3 tbsp olive oil
1 small handful fresh flat leaf
   parsley, roughly chopped, plus
   extra to garnish
1 garlic clove, crushed
350g/12oz ripe Italian plum
   tomatoes, peeled and chopped
60–90ml/4–6 tbsp dry
   white wine
350g/12oz fresh or dried linguine
salt and ground black pepper

1 Put the crabmeat in a mortar and pound to a rough pulp with a pestle. If you do not have a pestle and mortar, use a sturdy bowl and the end of a rolling pin. Set aside.

2 Heat 30ml/2 tbsp of the oil in a large pan. Add the parsley and garlic, with salt and pepper to taste, and fry for a few minutes until the garlic begins to brown.

3 Add the tomatoes, pounded crabmeat and wine, cover the pan and simmer gently for 15 minutes, stirring occasionally.

4 Meanwhile, cook the pasta until al dente. Drain well, reserving a few spoonfuls of the cooking water.

5 Return the pasta to the clean pan, add the remaining oil and toss quickly over medium heat to coat in oil. Add the crab mixture to the pasta and toss again, adding a little of the reserved cooking water if you think it necessary. Adjust the seasoning. Serve in warmed bowls, sprinkled with parsley.

> **Cook's Tip**
> *The best way to obtain crabmeat is to ask a fishmonger to remove it from the shell for you, or buy dressed crab from the supermarket. For this recipe you will need one large crab, and you should use both the white and dark meat.*

Capelli d'Angelo with Lobster

This is a sophisticated dish for a special occasion.

Serves 4
meat from the body, tail and
   claws of 1 cooked lobster
juice of ½ lemon
40g/1½oz/3 tbsp butter
4 fresh tarragon sprigs, leaves
   stripped and chopped
60ml/4 tbsp double
   (heavy) cream
90ml/6 tbsp sparkling dry
   white wine
60ml/4 tbsp fish stock
300g/11oz fresh capelli d'angelo
salt and ground black pepper
about 10ml/2 tsp lumpfish roe, to
   garnish (optional)

1 Cut the lobster meat into small pieces and put it in a bowl. Sprinkle with the lemon juice. Melt the butter in a large pan, add the lobster meat and tarragon and stir over the heat for a few seconds. Add the cream and stir for a few seconds more, then pour in the wine and stock, with salt and pepper to taste. Simmer for 2 minutes, then remove from the heat and cover.

2 Cook the pasta in lightly salted boiling water until al dente. Drain well, reserving a few spoonfuls of the cooking water.

3 Place the lobster sauce over medium to high heat, add the pasta and toss just long enough to combine and heat through; moisten with a little of the reserved water from the pasta. Serve in warmed bowls, sprinkled with lumpfish roe if you like.

> **Cook's Tip**
> *To remove the meat from a lobster, place the lobster on a board with its underbelly facing uppermost. With a large sharp knife, cut the lobster in half lengthways. Spoon out the liver and any pink roe (these can be eaten), then remove and discard the gills and stomach sac near the head. Pull the white tail meat out from the shell and discard the black intestinal vein. Crack the claws with a nutcracker and remove the meat from the base. Pull away the small pincer and remove the meat from this part of the shell. Pull the meat from the large pincer shell.*

Energy 549Kcal/2310kJ; Fat 19.6g; Saturated Fat 10.6g; Carbohydrate 56g; Fibre 2.2g

Energy 457Kcal/1932kJ; Fat 10.8g; Saturated Fat 1.5g; Carbohydrate 68g; Fibre 3.9g

Paglia e Fieno with Prawns & Vodka

The combination of prawns, vodka and pasta may seem unusual, but it has become something of a modern classic in Italy. Here it is stylishly presented with two-coloured pasta.

Serves 4
30ml/2 tbsp olive oil
1/4 large onion, finely chopped
1 garlic clove, crushed
15–30ml/1–2 tbsp sun-dried tomato paste
200ml/7fl oz/scant 1 cup panna da cucina or double (heavy) cream
350g/12oz fresh or dried paglia e fieno
12 large raw prawns (shrimp), peeled and chopped
30ml/2 tbsp vodka
salt and ground black pepper

1 Heat the oil in a medium pan, add the onion and garlic and cook gently, stirring frequently, for 5 minutes, until softened.

2 Add the tomato paste and stir for 1–2 minutes, then add the cream and bring to the boil, stirring. Season with salt and pepper to taste and let the sauce bubble until it starts to thicken slightly. Remove from the heat.

3 Bring a pan of lightly salted water to the boil and cook the pasta until al dente. When it is almost ready, add the prawns and vodka to the sauce; toss quickly over a medium heat for 2–3 minutes, until the prawns turn pink.

4 Drain the pasta well and turn into a warmed bowl. Pour the sauce over and toss to mix. Serve immediately.

Cook's Tip
The sauce is best served as soon as it is ready, otherwise the prawns will overcook and become tough. Make sure that the pasta has only a minute or two of cooking time left before adding the prawns to the sauce.

Energy 650Kcal/2722kJ; Fat 34.2g; Saturated Fat 17.7g; Carbohydrate 67.4g; Fibre 2.9g

Trenette with Shellfish

Colourful and delicious, this typical Genoese dish is ideal for a dinner party. The sauce is quite thin, so serve it with crusty bread and spoons as well as forks, so that nothing is missed.

Serves 4
45ml/3 tbsp olive oil
1 small onion, finely chopped
1 garlic clove, crushed
1/2 fresh red chilli, seeded and chopped
200g/7oz canned chopped Italian plum tomatoes
30ml/2 tbsp chopped fresh flat leaf parsley
400g/14oz fresh clams, in their shells
400g/14oz fresh mussels, in their shells
60ml/4 tbsp dry white wine
400g/14oz/3 1/2 cups dried trenette
a few fresh basil leaves
90g/3 1/2oz/2/3 cup peeled cooked prawns, (shrimp) thawed and thoroughly dried if frozen
salt and ground black pepper
chopped fresh herbs, to garnish

1 Heat 30ml/2 tbsp of the oil in a frying pan or medium pan. Add the onion, garlic and chilli and cook over medium heat for 1–2 minutes, stirring constantly. Stir in the tomatoes, half the parsley and pepper to taste. Bring to the boil, lower the heat, cover and simmer for 15 minutes.

2 Meanwhile, scrub the clams and mussels under cold running water. Discard any that are open or that do not close when sharply tapped against the work surface.

3 In a large pan, heat the remaining oil. Add the clams and mussels, with the rest of the parsley and toss over high heat for a few seconds. Pour in the wine, then cover tightly. Cook for about 5 minutes, shaking the pan frequently, until the clams and mussels have opened.

4 Remove the pan from the heat and transfer the clams and mussels to a bowl with a slotted spoon, discarding any shellfish that have failed to open.

5 Strain the cooking liquid into a measuring jug and set aside. Reserve eight clams and four mussels in their shells for the garnish, then remove the rest of the clams and mussels from their shells, adding any juices to the cooking liquid in the jug.

6 Bring a pan of lightly salted water to the boil, add the pasta and cook until al dente.

7 Meanwhile, add 120ml/4fl oz/1/2 cup of the reserved shellfish liquid to the tomato sauce. Bring to the boil over high heat, stirring. Lower the heat, tear the basil leaves and add with the prawns, the shelled clams and mussels. Stir well, then taste for seasoning.

8 Drain the pasta and turn it into a warmed bowl. Add the seafood sauce and toss well to combine.

9 Serve in individual bowls, sprinkle with herbs and garnish each portion with the reserved shellfish in their shells: two clams and one mussel per portion.

Energy 524Kcal/2218kJ; Fat 11.4g; Saturated Fat 1.7g; Carbohydrate 78.1g; Fibre 4g

Spaghetti with Anchovies & Olives

The strong flavours of this dish are typical of Sicilian cuisine. Serve with a hearty Italian red wine and chunks of rustic bread.

Serves 4

45ml/3 tbsp olive oil
1 large red (bell) pepper, seeded and chopped
1 small aubergine (eggplant), finely chopped
1 onion, finely chopped
8 ripe Italian plum tomatoes, peeled, seeded and finely chopped
2 garlic cloves, finely chopped
120ml/4fl oz/½ cup dry red or white wine
1 handful fresh herbs, such as basil, flat leaf parsley and rosemary
300g/11oz dried spaghetti
50g/2oz canned anchovies, roughly chopped, plus extra whole anchovies to garnish
12 pitted black olives
15–30ml/1–2 tbsp drained capers, to taste
salt and ground black pepper

1 Heat the oil in a pan and add the pepper, aubergine, onion, tomatoes and garlic. Cook gently, stirring frequently, for 10–15 minutes until the vegetables are soft.

2 Pour in the wine and 120ml/4fl oz/½ cup water, add the fresh herbs and pepper to taste and bring to the boil. Lower the heat and simmer, stirring occasionally, for 10–15 minutes.

3 Meanwhile, bring a pan of lightly salted water to the boil, add the pasta and cook until al dente.

4 Add the chopped anchovies, olives and capers to the sauce, heat through for a few minutes and taste for seasoning. Drain the pasta and turn it into a warmed bowl. Pour the sauce over the pasta, toss well and serve immediately.

> **Cook's Tip**
> *If the anchovies are omitted, this makes a good sauce for vegetarians. Serve with wholewheat spaghetti for extra fibre.*

Energy 509Kcal/2146kJ; Fat 15g; Saturated Fat 2.3g; Carbohydrate 76.5g; Fibre 7.8g

Penne with Cream & Smoked Salmon

This modern way of serving pasta is popular all over Italy. The three essential ingredients combine together beautifully, and the dish is very quick and easy to make.

Serves 4

350g/12oz/3 cups dried penne
115g/4oz thinly sliced smoked salmon
2–3 fresh thyme sprigs
25g/1oz/2 tbsp butter
150ml/¼ pint/⅔ cup single (light) cream
salt and ground black pepper

1 Bring a pan of lightly salted water to the boil, add the pasta and cook until al dente.

2 Meanwhile, using kitchen scissors, cut the smoked salmon into thin strips, about 5mm/¼in wide. Strip the leaves from the thyme sprigs.

3 Melt the butter in a large pan. Stir in the cream with about a quarter of the salmon and thyme leaves, then season with pepper. Heat gently for 3–4 minutes, stirring all the time. Do not allow the sauce to boil. Taste again for seasoning.

4 Drain the pasta, return to the pan, then toss in the cream and salmon sauce. Divide among four warmed bowls and top with the remaining salmon and thyme leaves. Serve hot.

> **Variations**
> *• Although penne is traditional with this sauce, it also goes very well with fresh ravioli stuffed with spinach and ricotta. This can be bought ready-made in most supermarkets.*
> *• The smoked salmon will cook to a mellow pink on contact with the hot sauce. Add it at the last minute if you prefer it raw.*
> *• Thyme dries well and 5ml/1 tsp may be used if you do not have any fresh thyme.*

Energy 475Kcal/2005kJ; Fat 17g; Saturated Fat 9g; Carbohydrate 67g; Fibre 2.7g

Saffron Pappardelle

Wide ribbon pasta not only looks attractive with this delicious seafood sauce, but it tastes fantastic, too. For an even prettier effect, use the type of pappardelle with a curly edge.

Serves 4

large pinch of saffron threads
4 sun-dried tomatoes, chopped
5ml/1 tsp fresh thyme
60ml/4 tbsp hot water
12 large prawns (shrimp) in their shells
225g/8oz baby squid
225g/8oz monkfish fillet
2–3 garlic cloves
2 small onions, quartered
1 small fennel bulb, trimmed and sliced
150ml/¼ pint/⅔ cup white wine
225g/8oz fresh or dried pappardelle
salt and ground black pepper
chopped fresh parsley, to garnish

1 Put the saffron threads, sun-dried tomatoes and thyme into a bowl and pour over the hot water. Mix together and then leave to soak for at least 30 minutes.

2 Wash the prawns and carefully remove the shells, leaving the heads and tails intact.

3 Pull the body from the squid, remove the quill and cut off the tentacles, then rinse. Pull off the outer skin and cut into 5mm/¼in rings. Cut the monkfish into 2.5cm/1in cubes.

4 Put the garlic, onions and fennel into a pan and pour over the wine. Cover and simmer for 5 minutes until tender.

5 Add the monkfish, with the saffron, tomatoes and thyme in their liquid. Cover and cook for 3 minutes. Then add the prawns and squid. Cover and cook gently for a further 1–2 minutes (do not overcook or the squid will become tough).

6 Meanwhile, bring a pan of lightly salted water to the boil and cook the past until al dente. Drain the pasta thoroughly.

7 Divide the pasta among four dishes and top each one with the seafood sauce. Sprinkle with parsley and serve immediately.

Energy 370Kcal/1566kJ; Fat 2.6g; Saturated Fat 0.4g; Carbohydrate 49.8g; Fibre 4g

Tagliatelle with Smoked Salmon

In Italy smoked salmon is imported, and therefore quite expensive. This elegant creamy sauce makes a little go a long way.

Serves 4–5

175g/6oz/¾ cup smoked salmon slices or ends, fresh or frozen
300ml/½ pint/1¼ cups single (light) cream
pinch of ground mace or nutmeg
350g/12oz dried green and white tagliatelle
salt and ground black pepper
45ml/3 tbsp chopped fresh chives, to garnish

1 Cut the salmon into thin strips about 5cm/2in long. Place in a bowl with the cream and the mace or nutmeg. Stir, cover, and allow to stand for at least 2 hours in a cool place.

2 Bring a pan of lightly salted water to the boil, add the pasta and cook until al dente.

3 Meanwhile, gently warm the cream and salmon mixture in a small pan without allowing it to boil.

4 Drain the cooked pasta and tranfer to a serving dish. Pour the sauce over the pasta and mix well. Season with salt and pepper and garnish with the chives. Serve immediately.

> **Cook's Tip**
> A mix of green and white pasta noodles is known as paglia e fieno, which translates as straw and hay.

> **Variation**
> For a quick spinach version, omit the marinating stage and simply stir the smoked salmon strips directly into the drained pasta with handfuls of baby spinach and some spoonfuls of crème fraîche. Stir over gentle heat until the salmon changes colour and the spinach begins to wilt. Add pepper and nutmeg.

Energy 415Kcal/1750kJ; Fat 14.6g; Saturated Fat 7.8g; Carbohydrate 53.4g; Fibre 2.5g

Salmon Rigatoni with Parsley Sauce

This dish is incredibly quick and easy to make and totally irresistible.

Serves 4
450g/1lb salmon fillet, skinned
225g/8oz/2 cups dried rigatoni
175g/6oz cherry tomatoes, halved
150ml/¼ pint/⅔ cup low-fat crème fraîche
45ml/3 tbsp finely chopped parsley
finely grated rind of ½ orange
salt and ground black pepper

1 Cut the salmon into bite-size pieces, arrange on a heatproof plate and cover with foil.

2 Bring a large pan of lightly salted water to the boil, add the pasta and bring back to the boil. Place the plate of salmon on top of the pan and simmer for 10–12 minutes, until the pasta and salmon are cooked.

3 Drain the pasta and toss with the tomatoes and salmon. In a separate bowl mix together the crème fraîche, parsley, orange rind and pepper to taste. Spoon this mixture over the salmon and pasta, toss well and serve hot or cold.

Variation
Fillets of fresh trout could be used instead, if salmon is unavailable.

Spaghetti with Bottarga

Although this may seem an unusual recipe, with bottarga (salted and air-dried mullet or tuna roe) as the principal ingredient, it is very well known in Sardinia, Sicily and parts of southern Italy. It is simplicity itself to make and tastes great. Bottarga can be bought from Italian delicatessens.

Serves 4
350g/12oz dried spaghetti
about 60ml/4 tbsp olive oil
2–3 garlic cloves, peeled
ground black pepper
60–90ml/4–6 tbsp bottarga

1 Cook the pasta in lightly salted water according to the instructions on the packet.

2 Meanwhile, heat half the olive oil in a large saucepan. Add the garlic and cook gently, stirring, for a few minutes. Remove the pan from the heat, scoop out the garlic with a slotted spoon and discard, leaving the garlic-flavoured oil in the bottom.

3 Drain the pasta thoroughly. Return the pan of oil to the heat and add the pasta. Toss well, season with pepper and moisten with the remaining oil, or more to taste.

4 Divide the pasta among four warmed bowls, sprinkle the grated bottarga over the top and serve immediately.

Top Energy 467Kcal/1962kJ; Fat 19.3g; Saturated Fat 6g; Carbohydrate 45g; Fibre 2.6g
Above Energy 419Kcal/1769kJ; Fat 13.4g; Saturated Fat 2g; Carbohydrate 66g; Fibre 2.9g

Penne with Tuna & Mozzarella

This tasty sauce is quickly made from kitchen cupboard staples, with the addition of fresh mozzarella.

Serves 4
400g/14oz/3½ cups dried penne, or other short pasta
15ml/1 tbsp capers, in brine or salt
2 garlic cloves
45ml/3 tbsp chopped fresh parsley
200g/7oz can tuna in olive oil, drained
75ml/5 tbsp olive oil
salt and ground black pepper
115g/4oz/⅔ cup mozzarella cheese, cut into small dice

1 Bring a large pan of lightly salted water to the boil, add the pasta and cook until al dente.

2 Meanwhile, rinse the capers well in water. Chop them finely with the garlic. Combine with the parsley and the tuna. Stir in the oil and season with salt and pepper, if necessary.

3 Drain the cooked pasta and turn it into a large frying pan. Add the tuna sauce and the diced mozzarella and cook over medium heat, stirring constantly, until the cheese just begins to melt. Serve immediately.

Cook's Tips
• *Use tuna canned in olive oil rather than brine, if possible.*
• *For this dish, cow's milk mozzarella is perfectly adequate, but if you are serving mozzarella uncooked, it is much better, and more traditional, to use the buffalo milk variety. The best is made around Naples and has a moist, springy texture and a deliciously milky flavour.*

Variation
Black or green olives could be used instead of capers; chop roughly and mix with the garlic, tuna, parsley and oil.

Energy 638kcal/2684kJ; Fat 26g; Saturated Fat 6.9g; Carbohydrate 74.4g; Fibre 3.5g

Spaghetti with Tomatoes, Anchovies, Olives & Capers

This classic sauce from Campania in the south uses strongly flavoured ingredients typical of the region. A few anchovies and olives give the sauce a punchy taste.

Serves 4

30ml/2 tbsp olive oil
1 small onion, finely chopped
1 garlic clove, finely chopped
4 canned anchovies, drained
50g/2oz/½ cup pitted black olives, sliced
15ml/1 tbsp capers
400g/14oz can chopped Italian plum tomatoes
15ml/1 tbsp chopped fresh flat leaf parsley
350g/12oz fresh or dried spaghetti
salt and ground black pepper

1 Heat the oil in a medium pan and add the onion, garlic and drained anchovies. Cook over low heat, stirring constantly, for 5–7 minutes, or until the anchovies break down to form a very soft pulp. Add the black olives and capers and stir-fry for a minute or so.

2 Add the tomatoes, 45ml/3tbsp water, half the parsley and salt and pepper to taste. Stir well and bring to the boil, then lower the heat and cover the pan. Simmer gently for 30 minutes, stirring occasionally.

3 Meanwhile, bring a pan of lightly salted water to the boil, add the pasta and cook until al dente.

4 Drain the pasta and transfer to a warmed bowl. Taste the sauce for seasoning, pour it over the pasta and toss well. Serve immediately, with the remaining parsley sprinkled on top.

> **Cook's Tip**
> Use good-quality, shiny black olives – the small Gaeta olives from Liguria are among the best of the Italian crop.

Spaghetti with Tuna, Anchovies, Olives & Mozzarella

This recipe from Capri is fresh, light and full of flavour, just like the beautiful island itself. Serve the dish as soon as it is cooked to enjoy it at its best.

Serves 4

300g/11oz dried spaghetti
30ml/2 tbsp olive oil
6 ripe Italian plum tomatoes, chopped
5ml/1 tsp sugar
50g/2oz jar anchovies in olive oil, drained
about 60 ml/4 tbsp dry white wine
200g/7oz can tuna in olive oil, drained
50g/2oz/½ cup pitted black olives, quartered lengthways
125g/4½oz mozzarella cheese, drained and diced
salt and ground black pepper
fresh basil leaves, to garnish

1 Bring a pan of lightly salted water to the boil, add the pasta and cook until al dente.

2 Meanwhile, heat the oil in a medium pan. Add the chopped tomatoes, sugar and pepper to taste, and toss over medium heat for a few minutes, until the tomatoes soften and the juices run. Using kitchen scissors, snip a few anchovies at a time into the pan of tomatoes.

3 Add the wine, tuna and olives and stir once or twice until they are just evenly mixed into the sauce. Add the mozzarella and heat through without stirring. Taste; add salt if necessary.

4 Drain the pasta well and transfer to a warmed serving dish. Pour the sauce over, toss gently and sprinkle with basil leaves. Serve immediately.

> **Cook's Tip**
> In Italy, anchovy fillets are preserved in salt as well as oil. The salted fillets have a superior flavour and are worth looking for.

Energy 390Kcal/1650kJ; Fat 9.1g; Saturated Fat 1.3g; Carbohydrate 69.1g; Fibre 4.1g

Energy 557Kcal/2346kJ; Fat 20.8g; Saturated Fat 6.6g; Carbohydrate 61.4g; Fibre 4g

Orecchiette with Anchovies & Broccoli

With its robust flavours, this pasta dish is typical of southern Italian cooking: anchovies, pine nuts, garlic and Pecorino are all popular.

Serves 4

300g/11oz/2 cups broccoli florets
40g/1½oz/½ cup pine nuts
350g/12oz/3 cups dried orecchiette
60ml/4 tbsp olive oil
1 small red onion, thinly sliced
50g/2oz jar anchovies in olive oil
1 garlic clove, crushed
50g/2oz/⅔ cup freshly grated Pecorino cheese
salt and ground black pepper

1 Break the broccoli florets into small sprigs and cut off the stalks: slice large stalks. Cook the broccoli florets and stalks in a pan of boiling salted water for 2 minutes, then drain and refresh under cold running water. Leave to drain on kitchen paper.

2 Put the pine nuts in a dry non-stick frying pan and toss over low to medium heat for 1–2 minutes, or until the nuts are lightly toasted and golden. Remove and set aside.

3 Cook the pasta in boiling water until al dente. Meanwhile, heat the oil in a frying pan, add the onion and fry gently, stirring frequently, for about 5 minutes, until softened. Add the anchovies with their oil, then the garlic and cook, stirring frequently, for 1–2 minutes, until the anchovies break down to a paste. Add the broccoli and plenty of pepper. Toss over heat for 1–2 minutes, until the broccoli is hot. Taste for seasoning.

4 Drain the pasta and turn into a warmed bowl. Add the broccoli mixture and grated Pecorino and toss well to combine. Sprinkle the pine nuts over the top and serve immediately.

Cook's Tip
Orecchiette (little ears) from Puglia are a special type of pasta with a chewy texture. You can use conchiglie instead, if wished.

Farfalle with Tuna

This quick dish makes a good weekday supper if you have canned tomatoes and tuna in the store-cupboard.

Serves 4

30ml/2 tbsp olive oil
1 small onion, finely chopped
1 garlic clove, finely chopped
400g/14oz can chopped Italian plum tomatoes
45ml/3 tbsp dry white wine
8–10 pitted black olives, cut into rings
10ml/2 tsp chopped fresh oregano or 5ml/1 tsp dried oregano, plus extra fresh oregano to garnish
400g/14oz/3½ cups dried farfalle
175g/6oz canned tuna in olive oil
salt and ground black pepper

1 Heat the olive oil in a medium frying pan or pan, add the onion and garlic and fry gently for 2–3 minutes, until the onion is soft and golden.

2 Add the plum tomatoes to the pan and bring to the boil, then pour over the white wine and simmer the mixture for a minute or so. Stir in the olives and oregano, with salt and pepper to taste, then cover and cook for 20–25 minutes, stirring from time to time.

3 Meanwhile, bring a pan of lightly salted water to the boil, add the pasta and cook until al dente.

4 Drain the canned tuna and flake it with a fork. Add the tuna to the sauce with about 60ml/4 tbsp of the water used for cooking the pasta. Taste and adjust the seasoning.

5 Drain the cooked pasta well and transfer to a warmed large serving bowl. Pour the tuna sauce over the top and toss to mix. Serve immediately, garnished with sprigs of oregano.

Variation
If you are cooking for children, try adding some canned corn to give the dish colour and a different texture.

Energy 578Kcal/2425kJ; Fat 25.5g; Saturated Fat 5.1g; Carbohydrate 67.8g; Fibre 4.9g

Energy 514Kcal/2174kJ; Fat 12.4g; Saturated Fat 1.9g; Carbohydrate 78.7g; Fibre 4.8g

Tagliatelle with Bolognese Sauce

This authentic ragù from the city of Bologna in Emilia-Romagna, central Italy, is traditionally served with tagliatelle.

Serves 6–8
450g/1lb fresh or dried tagliatelle
salt and ground black pepper
freshly grated Parmesan cheese,
   to serve

For the ragù
25g/1oz/2 tbsp butter
15ml/1 tbsp olive oil
1 onion, finely chopped
2 garlic cloves, finely chopped
2 carrots, finely chopped
2 celery sticks, finely chopped
130g/4¹⁄₂oz pancetta or rindless
   streaky (fatty) bacon, diced
250g/9oz lean minced (ground) beef
250g/9oz lean minced (ground) pork
120ml/4fl oz/¹⁄₂ cup dry
   white wine
2 x 400g/14oz cans crushed
   Italian plum tomatoes
475–750ml/16fl oz–1¹⁄₄
   pints/2–3 cups beef stock
100ml/3¹⁄₂fl oz/scant ¹⁄₂ cup
   panna da cucina or double
   (heavy) cream

1 Make the ragù first. Heat the butter and oil in a large pan until sizzling. Add the onion, garlic, vegetables and the pancetta or bacon and cook over medium heat, stirring frequently, for 10 minutes, or until the vegetables have softened.

2 Add the minced beef and pork, lower the heat and cook gently for 10 minutes, stirring frequently and breaking up any lumps in the meat with a wooden spoon. Stir in salt and pepper to taste, then add the wine and stir again. Simmer for about 5 minutes, or until reduced.

3 Add the tomatoes and 250ml/8fl oz/1 cup of the beef stock and bring to the boil. Stir well, then lower the heat. Half cover the pan with a lid and simmer very gently for 2 hours, stirring occasionally and adding more stock as it becomes absorbed.

4 Stir in the cream, then simmer, without a lid, for another 30 minutes, stirring frequently. Meanwhile, cook the pasta in boiling water until al dente. Taste for seasoning. Drain the pasta and transfer to a warmed bowl. Pour the sauce over the pasta and toss well. Serve immediately, sprinkled with Parmesan.

Energy 491Kcal/2058kJ; Fat 24g; Saturated Fat 10.9g; Carbohydrate 46.8g; Fibre 3.1g

Spaghetti with Meatballs

Mouthwatering meatballs simmered in a piquant tomato sauce are perfect with spaghetti or linguine.

Serves 6–8
350g/12oz minced (ground) beef
1 egg
60ml/4 tbsp roughly chopped
   fresh flat leaf parsley
2.5ml/¹⁄₂ tsp crushed dried
   red chillies
1 thick slice white bread, crusts
removed and torn into pieces
30ml/2 tbsp milk
about 30ml/2 tbsp olive oil
300ml/¹⁄₂ pint/1¹⁄₄ cups passata
   (bottled, strained tomatoes)
400ml/14fl oz/1²⁄₃ cups
   vegetable stock
5ml/1 tsp sugar
350–450g/12oz–1lb fresh or
   dried spaghetti
salt and ground black pepper
freshly grated Parmesan cheese,
   to serve

1 Put the beef in a large bowl. Add the egg and half the parsley and crushed chillies. Season with plenty of salt and pepper.

2 Place the bread in a small bowl. Moisten with the milk. Leave to soak for a few minutes, then squeeze out the excess milk and crumble the bread over the meat mixture. Mix well with a wooden spoon, then use your hands to squeeze and knead the mixture so that it becomes smooth and quite sticky.

3 Wash your hands, rinse them under the cold tap, then pick up small pieces of the mixture and roll them between your palms to make about 60 very small balls. Place the meatballs on a tray and chill for about 30 minutes.

4 Heat the oil in a large, deep non-stick frying pan. Cook the meatballs in batches until browned all over. Pour the passata and stock into the pan. Heat gently, then add the remaining chillies and the sugar, with salt and pepper to taste. Return all the meatballs to the pan. Bring to the boil, lower the heat and cover. Simmer for 20 minutes.

5 Cook the pasta until al dente, then drain and transfer to a warm large bowl. Pour the sauce over and toss gently. Sprinkle with the remaining parsley and serve with grated Parmesan.

Energy 324Kcal/1364kJ; Fat 11.6g; Saturated Fat 3.8g; Carbohydrate 40.3g; Fibre 2.7g

Rigatoni with Bresaola & Peppers

Bresaola – cured raw beef – is usually served thinly sliced as an antipasto. Here its strong, almost gamey, flavour is used to good effect in a sauce for pasta.

Serves 6
30ml/2 tbsp olive oil
1 small onion, finely chopped
150g/5oz bresaola, cut into
   thin strips
1 small handful fresh basil leaves
4 (bell) peppers (red and orange
   or yellow), seeded and diced
120ml/4fl oz/½ cup dry
   white wine
400g/14oz can chopped Italian
   plum tomatoes
450g/1lb/4 cups dried rigatoni
50g/2oz/²/₃ cup freshly shaved
   Parmesan cheese
salt and ground black pepper
fresh basil leaves, to garnish

1 Heat the oil in a medium pan, add the onion and bresaola. Cover the pan and cook over low heat for 5–8 minutes, until the onion has softened.

2 Stir in the basil leaves, then add the peppers, wine, 5ml/1 tsp salt and plenty of pepper. Stir well, then simmer gently for 10–15 minutes.

3 Add the canned tomatoes to the pan and increase the heat to high. Bring to the boil, stirring, then lower the heat and replace the lid again. Simmer gently, stirring occasionally, for 20 minutes or until the peppers are very soft and quite creamy.

4 Meanwhile, bring a pan of lightly salted water to the boil, add the pasta and cook until al dente.

5 Drain the cooked pasta and turn into a warmed bowl. Taste the sauce for seasoning, then pour it over the pasta and add half the Parmesan. Toss well, garnish with basil leaves and serve immediately, with the remaining Parmesan sprinkled on top.

> **Variation**
> Use pancetta or streaky (fatty) bacon instead of the bresaola.

Tagliatelle with Red Wine Bolognese Sauce

This is a versatile meat sauce. Here the quantity is also enough for 450g/1lb short shapes, such as penne.

Serves 4–6
1 onion
1 small carrot
1 celery stick
2 garlic cloves
45ml/3 tbsp olive oil
400g/14oz minced (ground) beef
120ml/4fl oz/½ cup red wine
200ml/7fl oz/scant 1 cup passata
   (bottled, strained tomatoes)
15ml/1 tbsp tomato purée (paste)
5ml/1 tsp dried oregano
15ml/1 tbsp chopped fresh flat
   leaf parsley
350ml/12fl oz/1½ cups beef
   stock
8 baby Italian tomatoes (optional)
450g/1lb/4 cups dried tagliatelle
salt and ground black pepper

1 Chop all the vegetables finely, either in a food processor or by hand. Heat the oil in a large pan, add the finely chopped vegetable mixture and cook over low heat, stirring frequently, for 5–7 minutes.

2 Add the minced beef and cook for 5 minutes, stirring frequently and breaking up any lumps in the meat with a wooden spoon. Stir in the wine and mix well.

3 Cook for 1–2 minutes, then add the passata, tomato purée, herbs and 60ml/4 tbsp of the stock. Season with salt and pepper to taste. Stir well and bring to the boil.

4 Cover the pan and cook over gentle heat for 30 minutes, stirring from time to time and adding more stock as necessary. Add the tomatoes, if using, and simmer for 5–10 minutes more.

5 Meanwhile, bring a pan of lightly salted water to the boil, add the pasta and cook until al dente.

6 Drain the pasta thoroughly and turn into a warmed serving bowl. Taste the sauce for seasoning, then add to the pasta and and toss to combine. Serve immediately.

Energy 228Kcal/946kJ; Fat 16.4g; Saturated Fat 5.4g; Carbohydrate 3.2g; Fibre 0.8g

Energy 391Kcal/1651kJ; Fat 9.1g; Saturated Fat 2.8g; Carbohydrate 60.1g; Fibre 4.6g

Fusilli Lunghi with Pepperoni

Long spiral pasta with a tangy sausage sauce makes a warming dish.

Serves 4

1 red (bell) pepper
1 green (bell) pepper
30ml/2 tbsp olive oil, plus extra
   for tossing the pasta
1 onion, chopped

2 x 400g/14oz cans chopped
   Italian plum tomatoes
30ml/2 tbsp tomato purée (paste)
10ml/2 tsp paprika
175g/6oz pepperoni or
   chorizo sausage
45ml/3 tbsp chopped
   fresh parsley
400g/14oz dried fusilli lunghi
salt and ground black pepper

1 Halve, core and seed the peppers. Cut the flesh into dice.

2 Heat the oil in a medium pan, add the onion and cook for 2–3 minutes, until beginning to colour and soften; do not allow them to turn brown.

3 Add the peppers, tomatoes, tomato purée and paprika to the pan and bring to the boil. Simmer, uncovered, for about 15–20 minutes, until reduced and thickened.

4 Slice the pepperoni or chorizo and stir into the sauce with 30ml/2 tbsp of the chopped parsley. Season to taste with salt and pepper.

5 While the sauce is simmering, bring a pan of lightly salted water to the boil, add the pasta and cook until al dente.

6 Drain the pasta well and turn into a bowl. Add the remaining parsley and toss together with a little extra olive oil. Divide among four warmed bowls and top with the prepared sauce.

> **Cook's Tip**
> *All types of sausage are suitable for this dish, but if using raw Italian sausages, such as Luganega, add them with the onion to cook through or cook separately, then cut into bite-size chunks.*

Energy 655Kcal/2756kJ; Fat 25.6g; Saturated Fat 7.7g; Carbohydrate 87.5g; Fibre 7.1g

Tagliatelle with Prosciutto & Parmesan

Consisting of a few prime Italian ingredients, this pasta dish is simplicity itself to make yet tastes wonderful. Serve with a fresh salad and chunks of ciabatta for lunch.

Serves 4

115g/4oz prosciutto
400g/14oz fresh or dried tagliatelle
75g/3oz/6 tbsp butter
50g/2oz/⅔ cup freshly grated
   Parmesan cheese
salt and ground black pepper
a few fresh sage leaves, to garnish

1 Cut the prosciutto into strips the same width as the tagliatelle. Bring a pan of lightly salted water to the boil, add the pasta and cook until al dente.

2 Meanwhile, melt the butter gently in a pan, stir in the prosciutto strips and heat through over very gentle heat, being careful not to let them colour.

3 Drain the tagliatelle through a colander and pile into a warmed serving dish.

4 Sprinkle the Parmesan cheese over the pasta and pour the buttery prosciutto on the top. Season well with black pepper and garnish with the sage leaves.

> **Cook's Tip**
> *Both fresh and dried tagliatelle taste good with this sauce. The flat ribbons are usually 1cm/½in wide and the dried version is often sold folded into nests, which then unravel as they cook. For the best flavour, try making your own fresh tagliatelle from egg dough (see page 6). You could try different coloured tagliatelle: green pasta has cooked spinach added at the same time as the eggs, while the pink variety has tomato. The pasta can also be flavoured with mushrooms, beetroot (beets) or saffron strands infused in a little boiling water.*

Energy 569Kcal/2394kJ; Fat 22.3g; Saturated Fat 12.9g; Carbohydrate 74.5g; Fibre 2.9g

Rigatoni with Pork

This is an excellent meat sauce using minced pork rather than the more usual minced beef.

Serves 4

1 small onion
½ carrot
½ celery stick
2 garlic cloves
25g/1oz/2 tbsp butter
30ml/2 tbsp olive oil

150g/5oz minced (ground) pork
60ml/4 tbsp dry white wine
400g/14oz can chopped Italian
  plum tomatoes
a few fresh basil leaves, plus extra
  shredded basil leaves to garnish
400g/14oz/3½ cups
  dried rigatoni
salt and ground black pepper
freshly shaved Parmesan cheese,
  to serve

1 Chop all the fresh vegetables finely, either in a food processor or by hand. Heat the butter and oil in a large pan until just sizzling, add the chopped vegetables and cook over medium heat, stirring frequently, for 3–4 minutes.

2 Add the minced pork and cook gently for 2–3 minutes, breaking up any lumps in the meat with a wooden spoon.

3 Lower the heat and fry for 2–3 minutes, stirring frequently, then stir in the wine. Mix in the tomatoes, whole basil leaves, salt to taste and plenty of pepper. Bring to the boil, then lower the heat, cover and simmer for 40 minutes, stirring occasionally.

4 Cook the pasta in boiling water until al dente. Just before draining the pasta, add a ladleful or two of the cooking water to the sauce. Stir the sauce well, then taste for seasoning. Drain the pasta, toss with the sauce and serve sprinkled with shredded basil and shaved Parmesan.

> **Variation**
> To give the sauce a more intense flavour, soak 15g/½oz dried porcini mushrooms in 175ml/6fl oz/¾ cup warm water for 15–20 minutes, then drain, chop and add with the meat.

Bucatini with Sausage & Pancetta

This rich sauce makes a satisfying main course dish when teamed up with bucatini, a long, hollow pasta that looks like thin drinking straws when raw.

Serves 4

115g/4oz pork sausagemeat
  (bulk sausage), preferably
  salsiccia a metro
400g/14oz can Italian
plum tomatoes
15ml/1 tbsp olive oil
1 garlic clove, crushed
115g/4oz pancetta or rindless
  streaky (fatty) bacon, chopped
30ml/2 tbsp chopped fresh flat
  leaf parsley
400g/14oz dried bucatini
60–75ml/4–5 tbsp panna da
  cucina or double (heavy) cream
2 egg yolks
salt and ground black pepper

1 Remove any skin from the sausagemeat and break the meat up roughly with a knife. Purée the tomatoes in a food processor or blender.

2 Heat the oil in a medium frying pan or pan, add the garlic and fry over low heat for 1–2 minutes. Remove the garlic with a slotted spoon and discard it.

3 Add the pancetta and the sausagemeat and cook over medium heat for 3–4 minutes. Stir constantly to break up the sausagemeat — it will turn brown and look crumbly.

4 Add the puréed tomatoes to the pan with half the parsley and salt and pepper to taste. Stir well and bring to the boil, scraping up any sediment from the sausagemeat that has stuck to the bottom of the pan. Lower the heat, cover and simmer for 30 minutes, stirring occasionally. Taste for seasoning.

5 Meanwhile, bring a pan of lightly salted water to the boil, add the pasta and cook until al dente.

6 Put the cream and egg yolks in a warmed bowl and mix. Drain the pasta well, add to the cream mixture and toss to coat. Pour the sausagemeat sauce over the pasta and toss again. Serve sprinkled with the remaining parsley.

Energy 537Kcal/2264kJ; Fat 16.5g; Saturated Fat 5.7g; Carbohydrate 79.5g; Fibre 4.5g

Energy 657Kcal/2760kJ; Fat 29.6g; Saturated Fat 11.5g; Carbohydrate 80.2g; Fibre 4.2g

Fettuccine with Ham & Peas

This simple dish makes a very good first course for six people, or a main course for three to four. The ingredients are all easily found, so the recipe makes an ideal impromptu supper.

Serves 3–6

50g/2oz/¼ cup butter
1 small onion, finely chopped
200g/7oz/1¾ cups fresh or
   frozen peas
100ml/3½fl oz/scant ½ cup
   chicken stock
2.5ml/½ tsp sugar
175ml/6fl oz/¾ cup dry white
   wine
350g/12oz fresh fettuccine
75g/3oz piece cooked ham, cut
   into bite-size chunks
115g/4oz/1¼ cups freshly grated
   Parmesan cheese
salt and ground black pepper

1 Melt the butter in a medium pan, add the onion and cook over low heat for about 5 minutes, until softened but not coloured. Add the peas, stock and sugar, with salt and pepper to taste.

2 Bring to the boil, then lower the heat and simmer for 3–5 minutes, or until the peas are tender. Add the wine, increase the heat and boil until the wine has reduced.

3 Bring a pan of lightly salted water to the boil and add the pasta. When it is almost al dente, add the ham to the sauce, with about a third of the grated Parmesan. Heat through, stirring, then taste for seasoning.

4 Drain the pasta and turn into a warmed large bowl. Pour the sauce over the pasta and toss well. Serve immediately, sprinkled with the remaining grated Parmesan.

Cook's Tip
If you prefer to use fresh fettucine, it may be worth investing in a pasta machine which has rollers that thin out the dough and cutters for producing ribbons of different widths.

Linguine with Ham & Mascarpone

Mascarpone cheese masquerades as cream in this recipe. Its thick, unctuous consistency makes it perfect for sauces. Have the water boiling, ready for the pasta, before you start making the sauce, because everything cooks so quickly.

Serves 6

25g/1oz/2 tbsp butter
90g/3½ oz cooked ham, cut into
   thin strips
150g/5oz/⅔ cup mascarpone
   cheese
30ml/2 tbsp milk
45ml/3 tbsp freshly grated
   Parmesan cheese, plus extra
   to serve
500g/1¼lb fresh linguine
salt and ground black pepper

1 Melt the butter in a medium pan, add the ham, mascarpone and milk and stir well over low heat, until the mascarpone has melted. Add 15ml/1 tbsp of the grated Parmesan and plenty of pepper and stir well.

2 Bring a pan of lightly salted water to the boil, add the pasta and cook until al dente.

3 Drain the cooked pasta well and transfer to a warmed bowl. Pour the sauce over the pasta, add the remaining Parmesan and toss well until thoroughly combined.

4 Taste for seasoning and serve the pasta immediately, with more ground black pepper sprinkled on top and extra grated Parmesan handed around separately.

Cook's Tips
• *Linguine, meaning "little tongues", is a flat version of spaghetti and is good with a wide range of sauces. You could also use spaghetti very successfully in this recipe.*
• *Mascarpone is a rich, thick cream cheese from Lombardy, with a texture similar to whipped cream. Made from cow's milk, it has a delicate flavour with a natural sweetness.*

Energy 412Kcal/1731kJ; Fat 15.1g; Saturated Fat 8.6g; Carbohydrate 48.1g; Fibre 3.4g

Energy 413Kcal/1745kJ; Fat 11.6g; Saturated Fat 6.4g; Carbohydrate 62.9g; Fibre 2.4g

Tortellini with Ham

Ready-prepared, fresh tortellini, enclosing tasty fillings, are now widely available. Combined with ham and tomato sauce, they make a delicious and instant Italian-style meal.

Serves 4
250g/9oz packet tortellini alla carne (meat-filled tortellini)
30ml/2 tbsp olive oil
¼ large onion, finely chopped
115g/4oz piece cooked ham, cut into bitesize chunks
150ml/¼ pint/⅔ cup passata (bottled, strained tomatoes)
100ml/3½fl oz/scant ½ cup panna da cucina or double (heavy) cream
about 90g/3½oz/generous 1 cup freshly grated Parmesan cheese
salt and ground black pepper

1 Cook the tortellini in plenty of boiling water.

2 Meanwhile, heat the oil in a large pan, add the onion and cook over low heat, stirring frequently, for about 5 minutes, until softened. Add the ham and cook, stirring occasionally, until it darkens.

3 Add the tomato passata. Fill the empty carton with water and pour it into the pan. Stir well, then add salt and pepper to taste. Bring to the boil, lower the heat and simmer the sauce for a few minutes, stirring occasionally, until it has reduced slightly. Stir the cream into the sauce.

4 Drain the pasta well and add to the sauce. Add a handful of grated Parmesan to the pan. Stir, then toss well and taste for seasoning. Serve in warmed individual bowls, topped with the remaining grated Parmesan.

Cook's Tips
• Passata is simply strained crushed tomatoes. Often sold in cartons, it is a handy shortcut for making quick sauces.
• Tortellini are small stuffed shapes, each made from a round of filled dough, folded in half and wrapped round into a ring.

Energy 350Kcal/1452kJ; Fat 28.6g; Saturated Fat 14.6g; Carbohydrate 7.2g; Fibre 0.6g

Pipe Rigate with Creamy Ham & Peas

Flecked with pink and green, this is a pretty dinner dish. The ridged, hollow pasta shapes not only look attractive, but are also ideal for trapping the prosciutto and peas inside.

Serves 4
25g/1oz/2 tbsp butter
15ml/1 tbsp olive oil
150–175g/5–6oz/1¼–1½ cups frozen peas, thawed
1 garlic clove, crushed
150ml/¼ pint/⅔ cup chicken stock, dry white wine or water
30ml/2 tbsp chopped fresh flat leaf parsley
175ml/6fl oz/¾ cup panna da cucina or double (heavy) cream
115g/4oz prosciutto, shredded
350g/12oz/3 cups dried pipe rigate
salt and ground black pepper
chopped fresh herbs, to garnish

1 Melt half the butter with the olive oil in a medium pan until foaming. Add the thawed frozen peas and the crushed garlic to the pan, followed by the chicken stock, wine or water.

2 Sprinkle in the chopped parsley and add salt and pepper to taste. Cook over medium heat, stirring frequently, for 5–8 minutes, or until most of the liquid has been absorbed.

3 Add about half the cream, increase the heat to high and let the cream bubble, stirring constantly, until it thickens and coats the peas. Remove from the heat, stir in the prosciutto and taste for seasoning.

4 Bring a pan of lightly salted water to the boil, add the pasta and cook until al dente.

5 Immediately melt the remaining butter with the rest of the cream in the pan in which the pasta was cooked. Add the pasta and toss over medium heat, until it is evenly coated.

6 Pour in the prosciutto sauce, toss lightly to mix with the pasta and heat through. Serve immediately, sprinkled with fresh herbs.

Energy 643Kcal/2693kJ; Fat 33.8g; Saturated Fat 18.5g; Carbohydrate 70.1g; Fibre 4.3g

Tagliatelle with Radicchio & Cream

This is a modern recipe that is very quick and easy to make. It is deliciously rich, and makes a good dinner party first course.

Serves 4
225g/8oz dried tagliatelle
75–90g/3–3½oz pancetta or streaky (fatty) bacon, diced
25g/1oz/2 tbsp butter
1 onion, finely chopped
1 garlic clove, crushed
1 head of radicchio, about 115–175g/4–6oz, finely shredded
150ml/¼ pint/⅔ cup panna da cucina or double (heavy) cream
50g/2oz/⅔ cup freshly grated Parmesan cheese
salt and ground black pepper

1 Bring a pan of lightly salted water to the boil, add the pasta and cook until al dente.

2 Meanwhile, put the pancetta or bacon in a medium pan and heat gently until the fat begins to run. Increase the heat slightly and fry the pancetta or bacon for a further 5 minutes, stirring frequently, until crisp and golden.

3 Add the butter, onion and garlic to the pan and cook for 5 minutes more, stirring. Add the radicchio and toss for 1–2 minutes until wilted.

4 Pour in the cream and add the grated Parmesan, with salt and pepper to taste. Stir for 1–2 minutes, until the cream is bubbling and well mixed in. Taste for seasoning.

5 Drain the pasta and transfer to a warmed bowl. Pour the sauce over and toss well. Serve immediately.

Cook's Tip
In Italy, cooks use a type of radicchio called radicchio di Treviso. It is very striking to look at, having long leaves that are dramatically striped in dark red and white. If you cannot get it, use the round radicchio instead, which is very easy to obtain.

Bucatini with Tomato & Chilli Sauce

This classic tomato sauce is called "Amatriciana" after the town of Amatrice in the Sabine hills, Lazio. If you visit Rome, you will see it on many menus served with either bucatini or spaghetti.

Serves 4
15ml/1 tbsp olive oil
1 small onion, finely sliced
115g/4oz smoked pancetta or rindless smoked streaky (fatty) bacon, diced
1 fresh red chilli, seeded and cut into thin strips
400g/14oz can chopped Italian plum tomatoes
30–45ml/2–3 tbsp dry white wine or water
350g/12oz/3 cups dried bucatini
30–45ml/2–3 tbsp freshly grated Pecorino cheese, plus extra to serve (optional)
salt and ground black pepper

1 Heat the oil in a medium pan and cook the onion, pancetta and chilli over low heat for 5–7 minutes, stirring. Add the tomatoes and wine or water, with salt and pepper to taste. Bring to the boil, stirring, then cover and simmer for 15–20 minutes, stirring occasionally. If the sauce becomes too dry, stir in a little water.

2 Meanwhile, bring a pan of lightly salted water to the boil, add the pasta and cook until al dente. Drain the pasta and turn it into a warmed bowl.

3 Taste the sauce for seasoning, pour it over the pasta and add the grated Pecorino. Toss well. Serve immediately, with more grated Pecorino handed around separately, if liked.

Cook's Tip
Always take care when dealing with chillies. They contain a substance called capsaicin, which will irritate delicate skin, so it's a good idea to wear rubber gloves when handling them.

Energy 543Kcal/2264kJ; Fat 35g; Saturated Fat 20g; Carbohydrate 44g; Fibre 2.1g

Energy 467Kcal/1972kJ; Fat 13.9g; Saturated Fat 4.6g; Carbohydrate 69.2g; Fibre 3.8g

Pork Meatballs with Corn Spaghetti & Tomato Sauce

This succulent recipe uses gluten-free corn spaghetti.

Serves 6

450g/1lb lean minced (ground) pork
1 leek, finely chopped
115g/4oz/1½ cups mushrooms, finely chopped
15ml/1 tbsp chopped fresh thyme
15ml/1 tbsp tomato purée
1 egg, beaten
30ml/2 tbsp potato flour
15ml/1 tbsp sunflower oil
350–500g/12oz–1¼lb fresh or dried corn spaghetti
fresh thyme sprigs, to garnish

For the tomato sauce

1 onion, finely chopped
1 carrot, finely chopped
1 celery stick, finely chopped
1 garlic clove, crushed
675g/1½lb ripe tomatoes, skinned, seeded and chopped
150ml/¼ pint/⅔ cup white wine
150ml/¼ pint/⅔ cup well-flavoured vegetable stock
15ml/1 tbsp tomato purée
15ml/1 tbsp chopped fresh basil
salt and ground black pepper

1 Preheat the oven to 180°C/350°F/Gas 4. Put the pork, leek, mushrooms, chopped thyme, tomato purée, egg and potato flour in a bowl and mix together. Shape into small balls, place on a plate, cover and chill.

2 Place all the sauce ingredients in a saucepan and season, then bring to the boil. Boil, uncovered, for 10 minutes, until thickened.

3 Heat the oil in a frying pan, add the meatballs and cook in batches until lightly browned.

4 Place the meatballs in a shallow, ovenproof dish and pour the sauce over. Cover and bake for 1 hour.

5 Meanwhile, cook the pasta in a pan of lightly salted, boiling water for 8–12 minutes, or according to the packet instructions, until al dente. Rinse under boiling water and drain. Divide the pasta into warmed bowls, spoon the meatballs and sauce over the top and serve garnished with fresh thyme.

Energy 425Kcal/1794kJ; Fat 11.8g; Saturated Fat 3.5g; Carbohydrate 54.2g; Fibre 4.5g

Spaghetti Carbonara

An all-time favourite that needs no introducing. This version has plenty of pancetta or bacon and is not too creamy, but you can vary the amounts as you please. Serve with a green salad and a smooth chianti.

Serves 4

30ml/2 tbsp olive oil
1 small onion, finely chopped
8 pancetta or rindless smoked streaky (fatty) bacon rashers (strips), cut into 1cm/½in strips
350g/12oz fresh or dried spaghetti
4 eggs
60ml/4 tbsp crème fraîche
60ml/4 tbsp freshly grated Parmesan cheese, plus extra to serve
salt and ground black pepper
fresh parsley sprigs, to garnish (optional)

1 Heat the oil in a large pan or frying pan, add the finely chopped onion and cook over low heat, stirring frequently, for about 5 minutes, until softened but not coloured.

2 Add the strips of pancetta or bacon to the onion in the pan and cook for about 10 minutes, stirring almost all of the time.

3 Meanwhile, bring a pan of lightly salted water to the boil, add the pasta and cook until al dente.

4 Put the eggs, crème fraîche and grated Parmesan in a bowl. Grind in plenty of pepper, then beat everything together well.

5 Drain the pasta, turn into the pan with the pancetta or bacon and toss well to mix. Turn the heat off under the pan. Immediately add the egg mixture and toss vigorously so that it cooks lightly and coats the pasta.

6 Taste for seasoning and adjust if necessary, then divide among four warmed individual bowls and garnish with parsley, if using. Serve immediately, with extra grated Parmesan handed around separately.

Energy 707Kcal/2964kJ; Fat 36.8g; Saturated Fat 14.3g; Carbohydrate 66.4g; Fibre 2.8g

Eliche with Sausage & Radicchio

Sausage and radicchio make a surprisingly delicious combination.

Serves 4
30ml/2 tbsp olive oil
1 onion, finely chopped
200g/7oz Italian pork sausage
175ml/6fl oz/³⁄₄ cup passata
  (bottled, strained tomatoes)
90ml/6 tbsp dry white wine
300g/11oz/2³⁄₄ cups dried eliche
50g/2oz radicchio leaves, finely
  shredded
salt and ground black pepper

1 Heat the olive oil in a large, pan. Add the finely chopped onion and cook over low heat, stirring frequently, for about 5 minutes, until softened.

2 Snip the end off the sausage skin and squeeze the sausagemeat into the pan. Stir the sausagemeat to mix it with the oil and onion and break it up into small pieces.

3 Continue to fry the mixture, increasing the heat if necessary, until the sausagemeat is brown and looks crumbly. Stir in the passata, then sprinkle in the wine and salt and pepper to taste. Simmer over low heat, stirring occasionally, for 10–12 minutes.

4 Meanwhile, bring a pan of lightly salted water to the boil and cook the pasta until al dente. Just before draining the pasta, add a ladleful or two of the cooking water to the sausage sauce and stir it in well. Taste the sauce to check the seasoning.

5 Drain the pasta and add to the sausage sauce. Add the radicchio and toss well to combine. Serve immediately.

> **Cook's Tips**
> • *The best sausage to use is called salsiccia puro suino, available from Italian delicatessens. It is made from 100 per cent pure pork plus flavourings and seasonings.*
> • *If you can get it, use the long, tapering radicchio di Treviso for this dish; otherwise the round radicchio can be used.*

Sardinian Sausage & Pasta

In Sardinia they call this dish simply "Malloreddus", which is the local name for the type of pasta traditionally used to make it. For authenticity, use sartizzu sardo sausage if you can find it.

Serves 4–6
30ml/2 tbsp olive oil
6 garlic cloves
200g/7oz Italian pure pork
  sausage, diced small
2 small handfuls fresh basil leaves
400g/14oz can chopped Italian
  plum tomatoes
a good pinch of saffron threads
15ml/1 tbsp sugar
350g/12oz/3 cups dried
  malloreddus (gnocchi sardi)
75g/3oz/1 cup freshly grated
  Pecorino sardo cheese
salt and ground black pepper

1 Heat the oil in a medium pan. Add the garlic, sausage and half the basil leaves. Fry, stirring frequently, until the sausage is browned all over.

2 Remove and discard the garlic. Add the tomatoes. Fill the empty can with water, pour into the pan, then stir in the saffron, sugar, 5ml/1 tsp salt and pepper to taste. Bring to the boil, lower the heat and simmer for 20–30 minutes, stirring occasionally.

3 Meanwhile, bring a pan of lightly salted water to the boil, add the pasta and cook until al dente.

4 Drain the pasta and turn into a warmed bowl. Taste the sauce for seasoning, pour over the pasta and toss well. Add one-third of the grated Pecorino and the remaining basil and toss well. Sprinkle with the remaining Pecorino and serve.

> **Cook's Tip**
> *In Sardinia, a special type of sausage is used for Malloreddus. It is flavoured with aniseed and black pepper and is called sartizzu sardo. A good alternative to sartizzu sardo would be the piquant salsiccia piccante. If, however, you prefer a slightly milder flavour, try luganega, which is more widely available.*

Energy 433Kcal/1817kJ; Fat 19.7g; Saturated Fat 7.3g; Carbohydrate 51.1g; Fibre 2.5g

Energy 518Kcal/2174kJ; Fat 23g; Saturated Fat 7.1g; Carbohydrate 63.2g; Fibre 3g

Pasta with Lamb & Peppers

This simple sauce is a speciality of the Abruzzo-Molise region, east of Rome, where it is traditionally served with maccheroni alla chitarra – square-shaped long macaroni.

Serves 4–6
60ml/4 tbsp olive oil
250g/9oz boneless lamb neck
    fillet, diced quite small
2 garlic cloves, finely chopped
2 bay leaves, torn
250ml/8fl oz/1 cup dry white wine
4 ripe Italian plum tomatoes, peeled
    and chopped
2 large red (bell) peppers, seeded
    and diced
400g/14oz/3 cups long pasta or
    maccheroni alla chitarra
salt and ground black pepper

1 Heat half the olive oil in a medium pan, add the lamb and season with a little salt and pepper. Cook over medium to high heat for about 10 minutes, stirring often, until browned.

2 Sprinkle in the garlic and add the bay leaves, then pour in the wine and let it bubble until reduced.

3 Add the remaining oil, the tomatoes and the peppers; stir to mix with the lamb. Season again. Cover with the lid and simmer over low heat for 45–55 minutes, or until the lamb is very tender. Stir occasionally during cooking and moisten with water if the sauce becomes too dry.

4 Meanwhile, cook the pasta until al dente, then drain. Remove the bay leaves from the sauce, then serve with the pasta.

Cook's Tips
• If you need to add water to the sauce towards the end of cooking, take it from the pan used for cooking the pasta.
• You can make your own fresh maccheroni alla chitarra or buy the dried pasta from an Italian delicatessen. Alternatively, this sauce is just as good with ordinary long or short macaroni. You will need 350–425g/12–15oz/3–4 cups.

Fusilli with Sausage

Spicy hot sausage and tomato sauce are married with spirals of pasta to make this really tasty dish from southern Italy. Pecorino cheese, with its strong and salty flavour, is the perfect accompaniment, along with a full-bodied red wine and country bread.

Serves 4
400g/14oz spicy pork sausages
30ml/2 tbsp olive oil
1 small onion, finely chopped
2 garlic cloves, crushed
1 large yellow (bell) pepper,
    seeded and cut into strips
5ml/1 tsp paprika
5ml/1 tsp dried mixed herbs
5–10ml/1–2 tsp chilli sauce
400g/14oz can Italian plum
    tomatoes
250–300ml/8–10fl oz/1–1¼
    cups vegetable stock
300g/11oz/2¾ cups fresh or
    dried fusilli
salt and ground black pepper
freshly grated Pecorino cheese,
    to serve

1 Grill (broil) the sausages for 10–12 minutes, until they are browned on all sides, then drain them on kitchen paper.

2 Heat the oil in a large frying pan or pan, add the onion and garlic and cook over low heat, stirring frequently, for 5–7 minutes, until soft. Add the yellow pepper, paprika, herbs and chilli sauce to taste. Cook gently for 5–7 minutes, stirring occasionally.

3 Add the tomatoes, breaking them up with a wooden spoon. Add salt and pepper to taste. Cook over medium heat for 10–12 minutes, adding the stock gradually as the sauce reduces.

4 While the tomato sauce is cooking, cut the grilled sausages diagonally into 1cm/½in pieces.

5 Add the sausage pieces to the sauce, reduce the heat to low and cook for 10 minutes. Meanwhile, cook the pasta in a pan of lightly salted water until al dente.

6 Taste and season the sauce. Drain the pasta and toss into the pan of sauce. Serve with Pecorino handed around separately.

Energy 704Kcal/2947kJ; Fat 39.4g; Saturated Fat 13.3g; Carbohydrate 71g; Fibre 4.4g

Energy 423Kcal/1783kJ; Fat 13.6g; Saturated Fat 3.5g; Carbohydrate 54.9g; Fibre 3.4g

Tagliatelle with Chicken & Herb Sauce

Chicken is enhanced with vermouth and herbs in this delicious creamy pasta dish.

Serves 4
30ml/2 tbsp olive oil
1 red onion, cut into wedges
350g/12oz fresh or
  dried tagliatelle
1 garlic clove, chopped
350g/12oz chicken breast fillets,
  skinned and diced
300ml/½ pint/1¼ cups
  dry vermouth
45ml/3 tbsp chopped fresh
  mixed herbs
150ml/¼ pint/⅔ cup
  fromage frais
salt and ground black pepper
shredded fresh mint, to garnish

1 Heat the oil in a large frying pan, add the red onion and fry for 10 minutes, until softened but not coloured and the layers have separated.

2 Bring a pan of lightly salted water to the boil, add the pasta and cook until al dente.

3 Add the garlic and chicken to the frying pan and fry for 10 minutes, stirring occasionally, until the chicken is browned all over and cooked through.

4 Pour in the vermouth, bring to boiling point and boil rapidly until reduced by about half. Stir in the herbs, fromage frais and salt and pepper to taste. Heat through gently, without allow the sauce to boil.

5 Drain the pasta thoroughly, transfer to a warmed serving dish and spoon the sauce over. Toss the mixture to coat the pasta. Serve immediately, garnished with shredded fresh mint.

Variation
Use mascarpone cheese, instead of fromage frais, if preferred.

Energy 571Kcal/2409kJ; Fat 11.1g; Saturated Fat 3.3g; Carbohydrate 69.9g; Fibre 2.8g

Fusilli with Chicken & Tomato

Just the job for a speedy dish – serve with a mixed bean salad.

Serves 4
15ml/1 tbsp olive oil
1 onion, chopped
1 carrot, chopped
50g/2oz drained sun-dried
  tomatoes in olive oil
1 garlic clove, chopped
400g/14oz can chopped Italian
  plum tomatoes, drained
15ml/1 tbsp tomato
  purée (paste)
150ml/¼ pint/⅔ cup
  chicken stock
350g/12oz/3 cups dried fusilli
225g/8oz chicken breast fillets,
  diagonally sliced
salt and ground black pepper
fresh mint sprigs, to garnish

1 Heat the oil in a large frying pan and fry the chopped onion and carrot for 5 minutes, stirring the vegetables occasionally.

2 Chop the sun-dried tomatoes and set aside until needed.

3 Stir the garlic, canned tomatoes, tomato purée and stock into the onions and carrots in the frying pan and bring to the boil. Simmer for 10 minutes, stirring occasionally.

4 Bring a pan of lightly salted water to the boil, add the pasta and cook until al dente.

5 Pour the sauce into a blender or food processor and process until smooth and well blended.

6 Return the sauce to the pan and stir in the sun-dried tomatoes and chicken. Bring back to the boil and then simmer for 10 minutes until the chicken is cooked. Adjust the seasoning.

7 Drain the pasta thoroughly and toss in the sauce. Serve at once, garnished with sprigs of fresh mint.

Cook's Tip
Try serving the sauce with a mix of white, green and pink fusilli.

Energy 433Kcal/1838kJ; Fat 6.6g; Saturated Fat 1g; Carbohydrate 72.4g; Fibre 4.6g

Piquant Chicken with Spaghetti

The addition of cucumber and tomatoes adds a deliciously fresh flavour to this unusual dish.

Serves 4

1 onion, finely chopped
1 carrot, diced
1 garlic clove, crushed
300ml/½ pint/1¼ cups
   vegetable stock
4 chicken breast fillets, skinned
bouquet garni
115g/4oz button mushrooms,
   thinly sliced
5ml/1 tsp wine vinegar or
   lemon juice
350g/12oz fresh or
   dried spaghetti
½ cucumber, peeled and cut
   into fingers
2 tomatoes, peeled, seeded
   and chopped
30ml/2 tbsp crème fraîche
15ml/1 tbsp chopped
   fresh parsley
15ml/1 tbsp snipped chives
salt and ground black pepper

1 Put the onion, carrot, garlic, vegetable stock, chicken and bouquet garni into a pan. Bring to the boil, cover and simmer for 15–20 minutes or until the chicken is tender. Transfer the chicken to a plate with a slotted spoon and cover with foil.

2 Strain the remaining cooking liquid in the pan. Discard the vegetables and return the liquid to the pan. Add the sliced mushrooms, wine vinegar or lemon juice, then stir and simmer for 2–3 minutes.

3 Bring a pan of lightly salted water to the boil, add the pasta and cook until al dente. Drain thoroughly.

4 Blanch the cucumber in boiling water for 10 seconds. Drain and rinse under cold water.

5 Cut the chicken breasts into bite-size pieces. Boil the stock to reduce by half, then add the chicken, tomatoes, crème fraîche, cucumber and herbs. Season with salt and pepper to taste.

6 Transfer the spaghetti to a warmed serving dish and cover with the piquant chicken and tomato sauce. Serve immediately.

Energy 315Kcal/1331kJ; Fat 5.6g; Saturated Fat 2.7g; Carbohydrate 26.6g; Fibre 2.6g

Chicken with Eliche & Olives

A delicious way to use up leftover cooked chicken, this colourful salad is fresh tasting yet satisfying.

Serves 4

225g/8oz cooked green beans
225g/8oz/2 cups mixed white, red
   and green dried eliche
1 beefsteak *tomato*
30ml/2 tbsp pesto sauce
15ml/1 tbsp olive oil
12 pitted black olives
350g/12oz cooked chicken, cubed
salt and ground black pepper
fresh basil, to garnish

1 Top and tail the green beans, then cut into 4cm/1½in lengths. Cook in a pan of lightly salted water until tender, then drain and refresh under cold running water. Drain again and set aside.

2 Bring a pan of lightly salted water to the boil, add the pasta and cook until al dente.

3 Meanwhile, plunge the tomato into a bowl of boiling water for 45 seconds, then plunge into a bowl of cold water for 30 seconds to loosen the skin. Slip off the skin. Halve the tomato and remove the seeds and core.

4 Drain the pasta and rinse in plenty of cold running water. Transfer the cooked pasta to a large bowl and pour in the pesto sauce and olive oil. Mix well to combine.

5 Cut the tomato into small cubes and add to the pasta mixture in the bowl with the olives and green beans. Season with salt and pepper and add the cubed chicken. Toss gently together and transfer to a serving platter or individual bowls. Garnish with fresh basil.

> **Cook's Tip**
> *Eliche shapes are similar to fusilli but have a slightly looser spiral: hence their name, which translates as "propeller". Alternatively, use the twisted fusilli casareccia instead.*

Energy 426Kcal/1794kJ; Fat 12.2g; Saturated Fat 2.2g; Carbohydrate 44.4g; Fibre 3.4g

Pasta with Chicken Livers

Rich-tasting chicken livers are coated in a piquant sauce and tossed with "little ears" in this appetizing dish.

Serves 4
225g/8oz chicken livers, defrosted if frozen
30ml/2 tbsp olive oil
2 garlic cloves, crushed
175g/6oz rindless smoked back bacon, roughly chopped
400g/14oz can chopped Italian plum tomatoes
150ml/¼ pint/⅔ cup chicken stock
15ml/1 tbsp tomato purée (paste)
15ml/1 tbsp dry sherry
30ml/2 tbsp chopped mixed fresh herbs, such as parsley, rosemary and basil
350g/12oz/3 cups dried orecchiette
salt and ground black pepper
freshly grated Parmesan cheese, to serve

1 Wash and trim the chicken livers. Cut into bitesize pieces. Heat the oil in a frying pan and fry the chicken livers for 3–4 minutes, until tender.

2 Add the garlic and bacon to the pan and fry until golden brown. Add the tomatoes, chicken stock, tomato purée, sherry, herbs and salt and pepper to taste.

3 Bring the sauce to the boil and simmer gently, uncovered, for about 5 minutes, until the sauce has thickened. Stir from time to time.

4 Meanwhile, bring a pan of lightly salted water to the boil, add the pasta and cook until al dente. Drain, then toss into the sauce. Serve hot, sprinkled with Parmesan cheese.

Cook's Tip
Chicken livers are popular for topping crostini as well as for pasta sauces. They also make a delicious salad when lightly sautéed, then tossed with salad leaves and dressed with hot olive oil from the pan, sizzled with vin santo (sweet Tuscan wine).

Energy 519Kcal/2187kJ; Fat 15.9g; Saturated Fat 4.2g; Carbohydrate 68.5g; Fibre 3.7g

Two-way Chicken & Vegetables

This tender slow-cooked chicken makes a tasty lunch or dinner, with the stock and remaining vegetables providing a nourishing soup as a second meal.

Serves 6
1.5 kg/3½ lb chicken
2 onions, quartered
3 carrots, thickly sliced
2 celery sticks, chopped
1 parsnip or turnip, thickly sliced
50 g/2 oz/½ cup button mushrooms, roughly chopped
1–2 fresh thyme sprigs or 5 ml/ 1 tsp dried thyme
4 bay leaves
1 large bunch of fresh parsley
sea salt and ground black pepper
cooked pasta and mangetouts (snow peas) or green beans, to serve

For the soup
115 g/4oz/1 cup dried wholewheat pasta shapes
chunks of crusty bread, to serve

1 Trim the chicken of any extra fat. Put it in a flameproof casserole and add the vegetables and herbs. Pour in water to cover. Bring to the boil over medium heat, skimming off any scum, then lower the heat and simmer for 2–3 hours.

2 Carve the meat neatly, discarding the skin and bones, but returning any small pieces of chicken to the pan. Serve the sliced chicken with some of the vegetables from the pan, plus the pasta of your choice and mangetouts or green beans.

3 Remove any large pieces of parsley and thyme from the pan, allow the remaining mixture to cool, then cover and chill in the refrigerator overnight.

4 To make the soup the next day, carefully lift off the fat that has solidified on the surface of the pan. Return the pan to medium heat and reheat the soup gently.

5 When the soup comes to the boil, add the pasta shapes, with salt to taste, and cook until the pasta is al dente. Season the soup with salt and plenty of ground black pepper and garnish with sprigs of fresh parsley. Serve with chunks of bread.

Energy 274Kcal/1156kJ; Fat 7.7g; Saturated Fat 1.3g; Carbohydrate 20.8g; Fibre 3.9g

Farfalle with Chicken & Cherry Tomatoes

Chicken flavoured with vermouth and herbs is cooked to succulent perfection in a tomato sauce with a hint of spiciness – unbeatable teamed up with bow-shaped pasta.

Serves 4

350g/12oz chicken breast fillets, skinned and cut into bitesize pieces
60ml/4 tbsp Italian dry vermouth
10ml/2 tsp chopped fresh rosemary, plus sprigs to garnish
15ml/1 tbsp olive oil
1 onion, finely chopped
90g/3½oz piece Italian salami, diced
275g/10oz/2½ cups dried farfalle
15ml/1 tbsp balsamic vinegar
400g/14oz can Italian cherry tomatoes
good pinch of crushed dried red chillies
salt and ground black pepper

1 Put the pieces of chicken in a large bowl, pour in the dry vermouth and sprinkle with half the chopped rosemary and salt and pepper to taste. Stir well and set aside.

2 Heat the oil in a large frying pan or pan, add the onion and salami and fry over medium heat for about 5 minutes, stirring frequently.

3 Bring a pan of lightly salted water to the boil, add the pasta and cook until al dente.

4 Add the chicken and vermouth to the onion and salami, increase the heat to high and fry for 3 minutes, or until the chicken is white on all sides. Sprinkle with the vinegar.

5 Add the cherry tomatoes and dried chillies. Stir well and simmer for a few minutes more. Taste the sauce for seasoning.

6 Drain the pasta and transfer to the pan. Add the remaining chopped rosemary and toss to mix the pasta and sauce together. Serve immediately, garnished with the rosemary sprigs.

Energy 490Kcal/2067kJ; Fat 14.1g; Saturated Fat 4.2g; Carbohydrate 55.8g; Fibre 3.2g

Penne with Chicken, Broccoli & Cheese

Broccoli, garlic and Gorgonzola meld together beautifully; a combination that complements the chicken very well in this sauce. Serve with tubular pasta to hold the sauce.

Serves 4

115g/4oz/scant 1 cup broccoli florets, divided into tiny sprigs
50g/2oz/¼ cup butter
2 chicken breast fillets, skinned and cut into thin strips
2 garlic cloves, crushed
400g/14oz/3½ cups dried penne
120ml/4fl oz/½ cup dry white wine
200ml/7fl oz/scant 1 cup panna da cucina or double (heavy) cream
90g/3½oz Gorgonzola cheese, rind removed and diced small
salt and ground black pepper
freshly grated Parmesan cheese, to serve

1 Plunge the broccoli into a pan of boiling salted water. Bring back to the boil and boil for 2 minutes, then drain in a colander and refresh under cold running water. Shake well to remove the surplus water and set aside to drain completely.

2 Melt the butter in a large pan, add the chicken and garlic, with salt and pepper to taste, and stir well. Fry over medium heat for 3 minutes, or until the chicken becomes white.

3 Meanwhile, bring a pan of lightly salted water to the boil and start to cook the pasta.

4 Pour the wine and cream over the chicken mixture in the pan, stir to mix, then simmer, stirring occasionally, for about 5 minutes, until the sauce has reduced and thickened. Add the broccoli, increase the heat and toss to heat the broccoli through and mix it with the chicken. Taste for seasoning.

5 Drain the pasta and transfer into the sauce. Add the Gorgonzola and toss well. Serve immediately, with freshly grated Parmesan cheese handed around separately.

Energy 869Kcal/3637kJ; Fat 46.5g; Saturated Fat 28g; Carbohydrate 75.7g; Fibre 3.7g

Pappardelle with Chicken & Mushrooms

Rich and creamy, this is a good dinner party dish.

Serves 4

15g/½oz dried porcini mushrooms
175ml/6fl oz/¾ cup warm water
25g/1oz/2 tbsp butter
1 small leek or 4 spring onions
  (scallions), chopped
1 garlic clove, crushed
1 small handful fresh flat leaf
  parsley, roughly chopped
120ml/4fl oz/½ cup dry
  white wine
250ml/8fl oz/1 cup chicken stock
400g/14oz fresh or dried
  pappardelle
2 chicken breast fillets, skinned
  and cut into thin strips
105ml/7 tbsp mascarpone
salt and ground black pepper
fresh basil leaves, shredded, to
  garnish

1 Put the dried mushrooms in a bowl. Pour in the warm water and leave to soak for 15–20 minutes. Turn into a fine sieve (strainer) set over a bowl and squeeze the mushrooms to release as much liquid as possible. Chop the mushrooms finely and set aside the strained soaking liquid until required.

2 Melt the butter in a medium frying pan, add the chopped mushrooms, leek or spring onions, garlic and parsley, with salt and pepper to taste. Cook over low heat, stirring frequently, for about 5 minutes, then pour in the wine and stock and bring to the boil. Lower the heat and simmer for about 5 minutes, or until the liquid has reduced and is thickened.

3 Meanwhile, cook the pasta in lightly salted boiling water, adding the reserved liquid from the mushrooms to the water.

4 Add the chicken to the sauce and simmer for 5 minutes, or until just tender. Add the mascarpone a spoonful at a time, stirring well after each addition, then add one or two spoonfuls of the pasta cooking water. Taste for seasoning.

5 Drain the pasta and transfer to a warmed large bowl. Add the chicken and sauce and toss. Serve, topped with the basil.

Energy 567Kcal/2397kJ; Fat 12g; Saturated Fat 6.2g; Carbohydrate 75.9g; Fibre 3.5g

Conchiglie with Chicken Livers & Herbs

Fresh herbs and chicken livers are a good combination, often used together on crostini in Tuscany. Here they are tossed with pasta shells to make a tasty supper dish.

Serves 4

50g/2oz/¼ cup butter
115g/4oz pancetta or rindless
  streaky (fatty) bacon, diced
250g/9oz frozen chicken livers,
  thawed, drained and diced
2 garlic cloves, crushed
10ml/2 tsp chopped fresh sage
300g/11oz/2¾ cups
  dried conchiglie
150ml/¼ pint/⅔ cup dry
  white wine
4 ripe Italian plum tomatoes,
  peeled and diced
15ml/1 tbsp chopped fresh flat
  leaf parsley
salt and ground black pepper
fresh parsley sprigs, to garnish
  (optional)

1 Melt half the butter in a medium frying pan or pan, add the pancetta or bacon and fry over medium heat for a few minutes, until it is lightly coloured but not crisp.

2 Add the diced chicken livers, garlic, half the fresh sage and plenty of pepper. Increase the heat and toss the livers for about 5 minutes, until they change colour all over.

3 Meanwhile, bring a pan of lightly salted water to the boil, add the pasta and cook until al dente.

4 Pour the wine over the chicken livers in the pan and let it sizzle, then lower the heat and simmer gently for 5 minutes.

5 Add the remaining butter to the pan. When it has melted, add the diced tomatoes, toss to mix, then add the remaining sage and the parsley. Stir well. Taste and add salt if needed.

6 Drain the pasta well and transfer to a warmed serving bowl. Pour the sauce over the pasta and toss well. Serve immediately, garnished with parsley sprigs, if liked.

Energy 528Kcal/2220kJ; Fat 20.2g; Saturated Fat 9.6g; Carbohydrate 59g; Fibre 3.2g

Spaghetti Bake with Turkey

An Italian-American recipe, this dish makes an excellent family meal. It is quite filling and rich, so serve it with a tossed green salad.

Serves 4–6

75g/3oz/6 tbsp butter
350g/12oz turkey breast fillet, cut into thin strips
2 pieces bottled roasted (bell) pepper, drained, rinsed, dried and cut into thin strips
175g/6oz dried spaghetti
50g/2oz/¹/₂ cup plain (all-purpose) flour
900ml/1¹/₂ pints/3³/₄ cups hot milk
115g/4oz/1¹/₄ cups freshly grated Parmesan cheese
1.25–2.5ml/¹/₄–¹/₂ tsp mustard powder
salt and ground black pepper

1 Melt about a third of the butter in a pan, add the turkey and sprinkle with a little salt and plenty of pepper. Toss the turkey over medium heat for about 5 minutes, until the meat turns white, then add the roasted pepper strips and toss to mix. Remove with a slotted spoon and set aside.

2 Preheat the oven to 180°C/350°F/Gas 4. Bring a pan of lightly salted water and cook the pasta until it is al dente.

3 Meanwhile, melt the remaining butter over low heat in the pan in which the turkey was cooked. Sprinkle in the flour and cook, stirring, for 1–2 minutes. Increase the heat to medium.

4 Add the hot milk a little at a time, whisking after each addition. Bring to the boil and cook, stirring, until the sauce is smooth and thick. Add two-thirds of the Parmesan, then whisk in the mustard, salt and pepper to taste. Remove from the heat.

5 Drain the pasta and return it to the clean pan. Mix in half the cheese sauce, then spoon the mixture around the edge of a baking dish. Stir the turkey mixture into the remaining cheese sauce and spoon into the centre of the dish. Sprinkle the remaining Parmesan evenly over the dish and bake for 15–20 minutes, until the cheese topping is just crisp.

Pappardelle with Rabbit Sauce

This rich-tasting dish comes from the north of Italy, where rabbit is popular.

Serves 4

15g/¹/₂oz dried porcini mushrooms
175ml/6fl oz/³/₄ cup warm water
1 small onion
¹/₂ carrot
¹/₂ celery stick
25g/1oz/2 tbsp butter
15ml/1 tbsp olive oil
40g/1¹/₂oz pancetta or rindless
streaky (fatty) bacon, chopped
15ml/1 tbsp roughly chopped fresh flat leaf parsley, plus extra to garnish
250g/9oz boneless rabbit meat
90ml/6 tbsp dry white wine
200g/7oz canned chopped Italian plum tomatoes or 200ml/7fl oz/scant 1 cup passata (bottled, strained tomatoes)
2 bay leaves, each torn once
300g/11oz dried pappardelle
salt and ground black pepper

1 Put the dried mushrooms in a bowl, pour over the warm water and leave to soak for 15–20 minutes. Finely chop the vegetables, either in a food processor or by hand.

2 Heat the butter and oil in a frying pan until just sizzling. Add the chopped vegetables, pancetta or bacon and the parsley and cook for about 5 minutes.

3 Add the pieces of rabbit and fry on both sides for 3–4 minutes. Pour the wine over and let it reduce for a few minutes, then add the tomatoes or passata. Drain the mushrooms and pour the soaking liquid into the pan. Chop the mushrooms and add them to the mixture, with the bay leaves and salt and pepper to taste. Stir well, cover and simmer for 35–40 minutes, until the rabbit is tender, stirring occasionally.

4 Remove the pan from the heat and lift out the pieces of rabbit with a slotted spoon. Cut them into bitesize chunks and stir them into the sauce. Remove and discard the bay leaves. Taste the sauce and add more salt and pepper, if needed.

5 Bring a pan of lightly salted water to the boil and cook the pasta until al dente. Meanwhile, reheat the sauce. Drain the pasta and toss with the sauce. Serve garnished with parsley.

Energy 473Kcal/1987kJ; Fat 20.8g; Saturated Fat 12.5g; Carbohydrate 36.3g; Fibre 1.4g

Energy 465Kcal/1961kJ; Fat 14.3g; Saturated Fat 5.7g; Carbohydrate 59.3g; Fibre 3.2g

Baked Vegetable Lasagne

A non-meat version of the classic favourite.

Serves 8
30ml/2 tbsp olive oil
1 onion, very finely chopped
500g/1¼lb tomatoes, fresh or
    canned, chopped
75g/3oz/6 tbsp butter
675g/1½lb cultivated or wild
    mushrooms, or a combination
    of both, wiped and sliced

2 garlic cloves, finely chopped
juice of ½ lemon
10–15 no pre-cook dried lasagne
    sheets
1 litre/1¾ pints/4 cups white
    sauce (see right)
175g/6oz/2 cups freshly grated
    Parmesan or Cheddar cheese
salt and ground black pepper

1 Butter a large shallow baking dish. In a small frying pan heat the oil and sauté the onion until soft but not coloured. Add the tomatoes and cook for about 6–8 minutes, stirring frequently. Season with salt and pepper and set aside until required.

2 Heat 40g/1½oz/3 tbsp of the butter in a frying pan, add the mushrooms and cook until they start to exude their juices. Add the garlic and lemon juice and season with salt and pepper. Cook until the liquids have almost all evaporated and the mushrooms are starting to brown. Set aside.

3 Make the white sauce as in step 4, right.

4 Preheat the oven to 200°C/400°F/Gas 6. Spread one large spoonful of the white sauce over the base of the dish. Top with a layer of pasta, cutting to fit. Cover with a layer of mushrooms, then one of white sauce. Sprinkle with a little cheese.

5 Make another layer of pasta, spread with a thin layer of tomatoes, then white sauce. Sprinkle with cheese. Repeat layering, ending with a layer of pasta coated with white sauce. Sprinkle with more cheese and dot with butter.

6 Bake for 20–30 minutes, until the pasta is tender. Remove from the oven and allow to stand for 5 minutes before serving.

Energy 466Kcal/1943kJ; Fat 28.7g; Saturated Fat 13g; Carbohydrate 34.8g; Fibre 2.6g

Mushroom & Courgette Lasagne

This is a great meat-free main course; the porcini give it a pronounced mushroomy flavour.

Serves 6
15g/½oz dried porcini mushrooms
175ml/6fl oz/¾ cup warm water
30ml/2 tbsp olive oil
75g/3oz/6 tbsp butter
450g/1lb courgettes (zucchini),
    thinly sliced
1 onion, finely chopped
450g/1lb/6 cups chestnut
    mushrooms, thinly sliced
2 garlic cloves, crushed
450g/1lb/2 cups ready-made
    tomato pasta sauce

10ml/2 tsp chopped fresh
    marjoram or 5ml/1 tsp dried
    marjoram
8–10 no pre-cook dried lasagne
    sheets
50g/2oz/⅔ cup freshly grated
    Parmesan cheese
salt and ground black pepper

For the white sauce
40g/1½oz/3 tbsp butter
40g/1½oz/⅓ cup plain
    (all-purpose) flour
900ml/1½ pints/3¾ cups hot
    milk
freshly grated nutmeg

1 Put the dried porcini in a bowl. Pour over the warm water and leave to soak for 15–20 minutes. Turn into a fine sieve (strainer) set over a bowl and squeeze the mushrooms to release as much liquid as possible. Chop finely and set aside. Strain the liquid and reserve half for the sauce.

2 Preheat the oven to 190°C/375°F/Gas 5. Heat the olive oil with 25g/1oz/2 tbsp of the butter in a large frying pan. Cook the courgettes, in two batches, in the pan, turning frequently, for 5–8 minutes, until lightly coloured. Remove from the pan with a slotted spoon and drain on kitchen paper.

3 Melt half the remaining butter in the pan, then cook the onion, stirring, for 1–2 minutes. Add half the fresh mushrooms and the garlic and season to taste. Toss over a high heat for 5 minutes, until tender. Transfer to a bowl with a slotted spoon, then repeat with the remaining butter and mushrooms.

4 To make the white sauce, melt the butter in a large pan, add the flour and cook, stirring, over medium heat for 1–2 minutes. Whisk in the hot milk gradually. Bring to the boil and cook, stirring, until the sauce is smooth and thick. Add nutmeg, salt and pepper to taste. Whisk well, then remove from the heat.

5 Place the tomato sauce in a blender or food processor with the reserved porcini soaking liquid and blend. Add the courgettes to the bowl of fried mushrooms, then stir in the porcini and marjoram.

6 Adjust the seasoning to taste, then spread a third of the tomato sauce in a baking dish. Add half the vegetable mixture, spreading evenly. Top with a third of the white sauce, then about half the lasagne sheets. Repeat these layers, then top with the remaining tomato sauce and white sauce and sprinkle with the grated Parmesan.

7 Bake the lasagne for 35–40 minutes, or until the pasta is tender. Stand for 10 minutes, before serving.

Energy 427Kcal/1784kJ; Fat 28.4g; Saturated Fat 14g; Carbohydrate 31.3g; Fibre 2g

Ravioli with Pumpkin

A tasty, less sweet version of the Christmas Eve speciality from Lombardy.

Serves 8
1 quantity handmade Egg Pasta (see page 6)
115g/4oz/½ cup butter
flour, for dusting
grated Parmesan cheese, to serve

For the filling
450g/1lb piece of pumpkin with skin, seeded and cut into chunks
15ml/1 tbsp olive oil
40g/1½oz/½ cup freshly grated Parmesan cheese
freshly grated nutmeg
salt and ground black pepper

1 To make the filling, preheat the oven to 220°C/425°F/Gas 7. Put the pumpkin, skin-side down, in a roasting pan and drizzle with oil. Roast in the oven for 30 minutes, turning twice. When cool enough to handle, scrape the flesh into a mixing bowl. Mash the pumpkin with a fork, then add the Parmesan with nutmeg, salt and pepper to taste. Stir well; set aside until cold.

2 Using a pasta machine, roll out one-quarter of the pasta into a 90cm–1m/36in–3 ft strip. Cut the strip into two 45–50cm/18–20in lengths. Using a teaspoon, put 10–12 little mounds of filling evenly along one side of one of the pasta strips.

3 Brush a little water around each mound, then fold the plain side of the pasta strip over the filling. Starting from the folded edge, press down gently around each mound, pushing the air out at the unfolded edge. Sprinkle lightly with flour.

4 With a fluted pasta wheel, cut along each long side, then in between each mound to make small square shapes. Put the ravioli on floured dish towels, sprinkle lightly with flour and leave to dry, while repeating the process to make 80–96 ravioli.

5 Drop the ravioli into a large pan of salted boiling water, bring back to the boil and boil for 4–5 minutes. Meanwhile, melt the butter in a small pan until it is sizzling. Drain the ravioli and divide between eight warmed plates. Drizzle the butter over the ravioli and serve with Parmesan.

Pansotti with Herbs & Cheese

This is a traditional dish from Liguria.

Serves 6–8
1 quantity handmade Egg Pasta (see page 6)
flour, for dusting
50g/2oz/¼ cup butter, melted
grated Parmesan cheese, to serve

For the filling
250g/9oz/1 cup ricotta cheese
150g/5oz/1½ cups grated Parmesan cheese

1 handful basil leaves, chopped
1 large handful fresh flat leaf parsley, chopped
a few marjoram sprigs, chopped
1 garlic clove, crushed
1 small egg
salt and ground black pepper

For the sauce
90g/3½oz shelled walnuts
1 garlic clove
60ml/4 tbsp extra virgin olive oil
125ml/4fl oz/½ cup panna da cucina or double (heavy) cream

1 To make the filling, put the ricotta, Parmesan, herbs, garlic and egg in a bowl with salt and pepper to taste. Beat well to mix.

2 To make the sauce, put the walnuts, garlic clove and oil in a food processor and process to a paste, adding up to 125ml/4fl oz/½ cup warm water through the feeder tube to slacken the consistency. Spoon the mixture into a large bowl and add the cream. Beat well to mix, then add salt and pepper to taste.

3 Using a pasta machine, roll out one-quarter of the pasta into a 90cm–1m/36in–3ft strip. Cut into two 45–50cm/18–20in lengths. Using a 5cm/2in square ravioli cutter, cut 8–10 squares from one pasta strip. Put a mound of filling in the centre of each.

4 Brush water around the edge of each square, then fold the square diagonally in half over the filling to make a triangle. Press to seal. Spread out the pansotti on floured dish towels and dust with flour. Repeat to make 64–80 pansotti.

5 Cook the pansotti in a pan of boiling water for 4–5 minutes. Put the walnut sauce in a warmed bowl with a little of the pasta water to thin it. Drain the pansotti and transfer to the bowl of walnut sauce. Drizzle butter over, toss and serve with Parmesan.

Energy 593Kcal/2475kJ; Fat 39.g; Saturated Fat 16.9g; Carbohydrate 43.3g; Fibre 2g

Energy 342Kcal/1435kJ; Fat 16g; Saturated Fat 8.9g; Carbohydrate 43g; Fibre 2.2g

Spinach & Ricotta Ravioli

The Italian name for this dish is ravioli di magro which means "lean ravioli". It describes the meat-free ravioli which are served on Christmas Eve.

Serves 8
1 quantity handmade Egg Pasta
  (see page 6)
flour, for dusting
freshly grated Parmesan cheese,
  to serve

For the filling
40g/1½oz/3 tbsp butter

175g/6oz fresh spinach leaves,
  trimmed, washed and shredded
200g/7oz/scant 1 cup ricotta
  cheese
25g/1oz/⅓ cup freshly grated
  Parmesan cheese
freshly grated nutmeg
1 small egg
salt and ground black pepper

For the sauce
50g/2oz/¼ cup butter
250ml/8fl oz/1 cup panna da
  cucina or double (heavy) cream
50g/2oz/⅔ cup freshly grated
  Parmesan cheese

1 To make the ravioli filling, melt the butter in a medium pan, add the spinach and salt and pepper to taste and cook over medium heat for 5–8 minutes, stirring frequently, until the spinach is wilted and tender. Increase the heat to high and stir to dry out.

2 Turn the spinach into a bowl and leave until cold, then add the ricotta, grated Parmesan and freshly grated nutmeg to taste. Beat well to mix, taste for seasoning, add the egg and beat well.

3 Using a pasta machine, roll out one-quarter of the pasta into a 90cm–1m/36in–3 ft strip. Cut the strip with a sharp knife into two 45–50cm/18–20in lengths (you can do this during rolling if the strip gets too long to manage).

4 Using a teaspoon, put 10–12 little mounds of the filling along one side of one of the pasta strips, spacing them evenly. Brush a little water around each mound, then fold the plain side of the pasta strip over the filling.

5 Starting from the folded edge, press down gently with your fingertips around each mound of filling, pushing the air out at the unfolded edge. Sprinkle lightly with flour.

6 With a fluted pasta wheel, cut along each long side, then in between each mound to make small square shapes. Put the ravioli on floured dish towels, sprinkle lightly with flour and leave to dry while repeating the process with the remaining pasta to get 80–96 ravioli altogether.

7 Drop the ravioli into a large pan of salted boiling water, bring back to the boil and boil for 4–5 minutes.

8 Meanwhile, make the sauce. Gently heat the butter, cream and Parmesan in a medium pan until they have melted.

9 Increase the heat and simmer for 1–2 minutes, until the sauce is slightly reduced, then season. Drain the ravioli and divide between large bowls. Drizzle the sauce over them and serve immediately, sprinkled with grated Parmesan.

Agnolotti with Taleggio

The filling for these little half-moons is very simple – only two ingredients – but the combination is stunning.

Serves 6–8
1 quantity handmade Egg Pasta
  (see page 6)
flour, for dusting

350–400g/12–14oz taleggio
  cheese
about 30ml/2 tbsp finely chopped
  fresh marjoram, plus extra
  to garnish
115g/4oz/½ cup butter
salt and ground black pepper
freshly grated Parmesan cheese,
  to serve

1 Using a pasta machine, roll out a quarter of the pasta into a 90cm–1m/36–3ft strip. Cut the strip with a sharp knife into two 45–50cm/18–20cm lengths.

2 Cut 8–10 little cubes of taleggio and place along one side of one of the pasta strips, spacing them evenly. Sprinkle each cube with a little chopped marjoram and pepper to taste.

3 Brush a little water around each cube of cheese, then fold the plain side of the pasta strip over them. Starting from the folded edge, press down gently with your fingertips around each cube, pushing the air out at the unfolded edge. Sprinkle lightly with flour.

4 Using only half of a 5cm/2in fluted round cutter, cut around each cube of cheese to make a half-moon shape. The folded edge should be the straight edge. Press the cut edges with the tines of a fork to give a decorative effect, if you like.

5 Put the agnolotti on floured dish towels, sprinkle with flour and leave to dry. Repeat the process to make 64–80 agnolotti.

6 Drop the agnolotti into a large pan of salted boiling water and cook for 4–5 minutes, until al dente. Meanwhile, melt the butter in a small pan until sizzling. Drain the pasta and divide between 6–8 warmed plates. Drizzle with the sizzling butter, garnish with chopped marjoram and serve with the freshly grated Parmesan.

Energy 483Kcal/2021kJ; Fat 27.2g; Saturated Fat 17.1g; Carbohydrate 42g; Fibre 1.9g

Energy 547Kcal/2283kJ; Fat 35.6g; Saturated Fat 21.5g; Carbohydrate 43.4g; Fibre 2.1g

Cannelloni Sorrentina-style

A delicious tomato-filled version of the classic dish.

Serves 4–6

60ml/4 tbsp olive oil
1 small onion, finely chopped
900g/2lb ripe Italian tomatoes, peeled and finely chopped
2 garlic cloves, crushed
1 large handful fresh basil leaves, shredded
250ml/8fl oz/1 cup vegetable stock
250ml/8fl oz/1 cup dry white wine
30ml/2 tbsp sun-dried tomato purée (paste)
2.5ml/½ tsp sugar
16–18 fresh or dried lasagne
250g/9oz/generous 1 cup ricotta cheese
130g/4½oz mozzarella cheese, drained and diced small
8 bottled anchovy fillets in olive oil, drained and halved lengthways
50g/2oz/⅔ cup freshly grated Parmesan cheese
salt and ground black pepper

1 Cook the onion in the oil for about 5 minutes, until softened. Stir in the tomatoes, garlic and half the basil. Season with salt and pepper to taste and cook for 5 minutes. Transfer half the tomato mixture to a bowl and allow to cool.

2 Stir the stock, wine, tomato purée and sugar into the mixture in the pan and simmer for 20 minutes, stirring, then purée.

3 Meanwhile, cook the lasagne sheets in batches in a pan of salted boiling water until *al dente*. Drain on clean dish towels.

4 Preheat the oven to 190°C/375°F/Gas 5. Add the cheeses to the tomatoes in the bowl. Stir in most of the remaining basil and season. Spread a little cheese mixture over each lasagne sheet. Place an anchovy fillet across the width of each sheet, close to one of the short ends, then roll up like a Swiss (jelly) roll.

5 Spread a little of the tomato sauce over the bottom of a large baking dish. Arrange the cannelloni seam-side down in a layer in the dish and spoon the remaining sauce over them.

6 Sprinkle the Parmesan over the top and bake for 20 minutes or until golden. Serve, garnished with the remaining basil leaves.

Energy 476Kcal/1995kJ; Fat 22.4g; Saturated Fat 9.9g; Carbohydrate 45g; Fibre 3.7g

Pasta Pie

A marvellous family dish, packed with Italian flavours.

Serves 4

30ml/2 tbsp olive oil
1 small onion, finely chopped
400g/14oz can chopped Italian plum tomatoes
15ml/1 tbsp sun-dried tomato purée (paste)
5ml/1 tsp dried mixed herbs
5ml/1 tsp dried oregano or basil
5ml/1 tsp sugar
175g/6oz/1½ cups dried conchiglie or rigatoni
30ml/2 tbsp freshly grated Parmesan cheese
30ml/2 tbsp dried breadcrumbs
salt and ground black pepper

For the white sauce
25g/1oz/2 tbsp butter
25g/1oz/¼ cup plain (all-purpose) flour
600ml/1 pint/2½ cups milk
1 egg

1 Heat the olive oil in a large frying pan and cook the onion gently for about 5 minutes, stirring, until softened. Stir in the tomatoes. Fill the empty can with water and add to the pan, with the tomato paste, herbs and sugar.

2 Add salt and pepper to taste and bring to the boil, stirring. Cover, lower the heat and simmer for 10–15 minutes.

3 Meanwhile, preheat the oven to 190°C/375°F/Gas 5. Cook the pasta in lightly salted boiling water until al dente.

4 Meanwhile, make the white sauce. Melt the butter in a pan, add the flour and cook, stirring, for 1 minute. Whisk in the milk gradually. Bring to the boil and cook, stirring, until the sauce is smooth and thick. Season, then remove the pan from the heat.

5 Drain the pasta and turn into a baking dish. Taste the tomato sauce for seasoning. Pour into the dish and stir well to mix.

6 Beat the egg into the white sauce, then pour the sauce over the pasta mixture. With a fork, separate the pasta in several places so that the white sauce fills the gaps. Sprinkle with the Parmesan and breadcrumbs and bake for 15–20 minutes, or until golden brown. Stand for about 10 minutes before serving.

Energy 444Kcal/1870kJ; Fat 18.4g; Saturated Fat 7.8g; Carbohydrate 56g; Fibre 3g

Spinach & Hazelnut Lasagne

Hazelnuts add a delicious crunchy texture to the spinach layer of this wholesome lasagne.

Serves 4

900g/2lb fresh spinach
300ml/½ pint/1¼ cups vegetable or chicken stock
1 onion, finely chopped
1 garlic clove, crushed
75g/3oz/¾ cup hazelnuts
30ml/2 tbsp chopped fresh basil
6–8 no pre-cook dried lasagne sheets
400g/14oz can chopped Italian plum tomatoes
200g/7oz/scant 1 cup mascarpone
flaked hazelnuts and chopped parsley, to garnish

1 Preheat the oven to 200°C/400°F/Gas 6. Wash the fresh spinach and place in a pan with just the water that clings to the leaves. Cook the spinach over fairly high heat for 2 minutes, until wilted. Drain well.

2 Heat 30ml/2 tbsp of the stock in a large pan and simmer the onion and garlic until soft. Stir in the spinach, hazelnuts and chopped fresh basil.

3 Arrange a layer of the spinach mixture in a large rectangular ovenproof dish, top with a layer of lasagne sheets, then spoon over a layer of chopped tomatoes, seasoning well with salt and pepper between the layers.

4 Continuing layering until the ingredients are used up. Pour over the remaining stock. Spread the mascarpone over the top.

5 Bake the lasagne for about 45 minutes or until golden brown. Serve hot, sprinkled with attractive lines of flaked hazelnuts and chopped fresh parsley.

> **Cook's Tip**
> If fresh spinach is unavailable, use frozen spinach instead – you will need 450g/1lb frozen.

Energy 474Kcal/1983kJ; Fat 22.3g; Saturated Fat 5.9g; Carbohydrate 50.4g; Fibre 9.1g

Leek & Goat's Cheese Lasagne

An unusual and lighter than average lasagne using a soft goat's cheese. The pasta sheets are not so chewy if boiled briefly first, or use no pre-cook lasagne instead, if you prefer.

Serves 6

8–10 lasagne sheets
1 large aubergine (eggplant), sliced
3 leeks, thinly sliced
30ml/2 tbsp olive oil
2 red (bell) peppers
200g/7oz goat's cheese, broken into pieces
50g/2oz/⅔ cup freshly grated Pecorino or Parmesan cheese

For the sauce
65g/2½oz/5 tbsp butter
65g/2½oz/9 tbsp plain (all-purpose) flour
900ml/1½ pints/3¾ cups milk
2.5ml/½ tsp ground bay leaves
freshly grated nutmeg
salt and ground black pepper

1 If necessary, blanch the pasta sheets in plenty of boiling water for just 2 minutes. Drain and place on a clean dish towel.

2 Lightly salt the aubergine slices and place in a colander to drain for 30 minutes, then rinse and pat dry with kitchen paper.

3 Preheat the oven to 190°C/375°F/Gas 5. Lightly fry the leeks in the oil until softened. Grill (broil) the peppers under a pre-heated grill (broiler) until charred. Cool in a covered bowl, then remove the skins, seeds and cores and cut into strips.

4 To make the sauce, melt the butter in a pan and add the flour. Cook, stirring, for 2–3 minutes. Add the milk and bring to the boil, stirring constantly until thickened. Add the bay leaves, nutmeg and salt and pepper to taste. Simmer for 2 minutes.

5 In a greased shallow casserole, layer the leeks, lasagne sheets, aubergine, goat's cheese and Pecorino or Parmesan. Trickle the sauce over the layers, distributing it over the entire dish.

6 Finish with a layer of sauce and grated cheese. Bake in the oven for 30 minutes, or until bubbling and browned on top.

Energy 524Kcal/2194kJ; Fat 28.1g; Saturated Fat 15.7g; Carbohydrate 47.9g; Fibre 5.1g

Baked Macaroni with Cheese

This delicious dish is perhaps less common in Italy than other pasta dishes, but has become a family favourite around the world.

Serves 6
475ml/16fl oz/2 cups milk
1 bay leaf
3 mace blades
50g/2oz/1¼ cups butter
40g/1½oz/⅓ cup plain (all-purpose) flour
175g/6oz/2 cups grated Parmesan or Cheddar cheese, or a combination of both
40g/1½oz/⅓ cup dry breadcrumbs
450g/1lb/4 cups short-cut macaroni
salt and ground black pepper

1 To make the white sauce, gently heat the milk with the bay leaf and mace in a small pan. Do not let it boil.

2 In a separate medium, heavy pan, melt the butter. Add the flour and mix in well with a wire whisk. Cook for 2–3 minutes, but do not let the butter burn.

3 Strain the hot milk into the flour and butter mixture all at once and mix smoothly with the whisk. Bring the sauce to the boil, stirring constantly, and simmer for a further 4–5 minutes.

4 Season with salt and pepper. Add all but 30ml/2 tbsp of the cheese and stir over low heat, until melted. Place a layer of clear film (plastic wrap) directly on the surface of the sauce to prevent a skin forming and set aside.

5 Preheat the oven to 200°C/400°F/Gas 6. Grease an ovenproof dish and sprinkle with some of the breadcrumbs.

6 Bring a pan of lightly salted water to the boil, add the pasta and cook until al dente.

7 Drain the pasta, and combine it with the sauce. Pour it into the prepared dish. Sprinkle the top with the remaining breadcrumbs and grated cheese and bake in the centre of the oven for 20 minutes, until golden and bubbling.

Energy 523Kcal/2202kJ; Fat 19.3g; Saturated Fat 11.7g; Carbohydrate 69.7g; Fibre 2.5g

Aubergine Lasagne

A tasty variation of the classic meat dish, this is a hearty, filling lasagne.

Serves 4
3 aubergines (eggplants), sliced
75ml/5 tbsp olive oil
2 large onions, finely chopped
2 x 400g/14oz cans chopped Italian plum tomatoes
5ml/1 tsp dried mixed herbs
2–3 garlic cloves, crushed
6 no pre-cook dried lasagne sheets
salt and ground black pepper

For the cheese sauce
25g/1oz/2 tbsp butter
25g/1oz/¼ cup plain (all-purpose) flour
300ml/½ pint/1¼ cups milk
2.5ml/½ tsp hot mustard
115g/4oz/1 cup grated mature Cheddar
15g/½oz/1 tbsp grated Parmesan cheese

1 Layer the sliced aubergine in a colander, sprinkling lightly with salt between each layer. Leave to stand for 1 hour, then rinse and pat dry with kitchen paper.

2 Heat 60ml/4 tbsp of the oil in a large pan, fry the aubergine and drain on kitchen paper. Add the remaining oil to the pan, cook the onions for 5 minutes, then stir in the tomatoes, herbs, garlic and salt and pepper. Bring to the boil and simmer, covered, for 30 minutes.

3 To make the cheese sauce, melt the butter in a pan, stir in the flour and cook gently for 1 minute, stirring. Gradually stir in the milk. Bring to the boil, stirring, and cook for 2 minutes. Remove from the heat and stir in the mustard, cheeses and seasoning.

4 Preheat the oven to 200°C/400°F/Gas 6. Arrange half the aubergines in the base of an ovenproof dish, and spoon half the tomato sauce over. Arrange three sheets of lasagne on top. Repeat this layering.

5 Spoon the cheese sauce over, cover and bake for 30 minutes, until lightly browned. Serve immediately.

Energy 541Kcal/2259kJ; Fat 32.7g; Saturated Fat 13.5g; Carbohydrate 44.4g; Fibre 7.3g

Cannelloni with Mixed Vegetables

This version of the classic beef-filled cannelloni introduces a variety of vegetables topped with cheese sauce.

Serves 4
8 dried cannelloni tubes
115g/4oz spinach
tomatoes and green salad, to serve (optional)

For the filling
15ml/1 tbsp oil
175g/6oz/³⁄₄ cup minced (ground) beef
2 garlic cloves, crushed
25g/1oz/¹⁄₄ cup plain (all-purpose) flour
120ml/4fl oz/¹⁄₂ cup beef stock
1 small carrot, finely chopped
1 small yellow courgette (zucchini), chopped
salt and ground black pepper

For the sauce
25g/1oz/2 tbsp butter
25g/1oz/¹⁄₄ cup plain (all-purpose) flour
250ml/8fl oz/1 cup milk
50g/2oz/²⁄₃ cup freshly grated Parmesan cheese

1 Preheat the oven to 180°C/350°F/Gas 4. To make the filling, heat the oil in a large pan. Add the minced beef and garlic, and cook for 5 minutes, stirring frequently.

2 Add the flour and cook for a further 1 minute. Slowly stir in the stock and bring to the boil, stirring. Add the carrot and courgette and season with salt and pepper to taste. Cook over medium heat for 10 minutes.

3 Carefully spoon the beef mixture into the cannelloni tubes and arrange in an ovenproof dish.

4 Blanch the spinach in boiling water for 3 minutes. Drain well and place on top of the cannelloni tubes in the dish.

5 To make the sauce, melt the butter in a pan. Add the flour and cook for 1 minute. Stir in the milk and cook, stirring, until smooth and thick. Add the grated cheese and season well.

6 Pour the sauce over the cannelloni and spinach and bake for 30 minutes. Serve with tomatoes and a green salad, if liked.

Energy 491Kcal/2062kJ; Fat 21.7g; Saturated Fat 10.2g; Carbohydrate 52.6g; Fibre 3.4g

Broccoli & Ricotta Cannelloni

Pine nuts lend a delicious crunch to this creamy dish.

Serves 4
60ml/4 tbsp olive oil, plus extra for brushing
12 dried cannelloni tubes
450g/1lb/4 cups broccoli florets
75g/3oz/1¹⁄₂ cups fresh breadcrumbs
150ml/¹⁄₄ pint/²⁄₃ cup milk
225g/8oz/1 cup ricotta cheese
pinch of freshly grated nutmeg
90ml/6 tbsp grated Parmesan
30ml/2 tbsp pine nuts
salt and ground black pepper

For the tomato sauce
30ml/2 tbsp olive oil
1 onion, finely chopped
1 garlic clove, crushed
2 x 400g/14oz cans chopped Italian plum tomatoes
15ml/1 tbsp tomato purée (paste)
4 black olives, pitted and chopped
5ml/1 tsp dried thyme

1 Preheat the oven to 190°C/375°F/Gas 5 and lightly grease an ovenproof dish with olive oil. Bring a large pan of water to the boil, add a little olive oil and simmer the cannelloni tubes, uncovered, for about 6–7 minutes, or until nearly cooked.

2 Meanwhile, steam or boil the broccoli for 10 minutes, until tender. Drain the pasta, rinse under cold water and reserve. Drain the broccoli and leave to cool, then place in a blender or food processor and process until smooth. Set aside.

3 Place the breadcrumbs in a bowl, add the milk and oil and stir until softened. Add the ricotta, broccoli purée, nutmeg, 60ml/4 tbsp of the Parmesan cheese and seasoning; set aside.

4 To make the sauce, heat the oil in a frying pan, add the onion and garlic and fry for 5–6 minutes, until softened but not brown. Stir in the tomatoes, tomato purée, black olives, thyme and seasoning. Boil rapidly for 2–3 minutes, then pour into the dish.

5 Spoon the cheese mixture into a piping bag fitted with a 1cm/¹⁄₂in nozzle. Standing each cannelloni tube upright on a board, pipe the filling into each tube. Lay in rows in the tomato sauce. Brush the tops with oil and sprinkle with the remaining Parmesan and pine nuts. Bake for 25–30 minutes until golden.

Energy 733Kcal/3074kJ; Fat 36.3g; Saturated Fat 13.1g; Carbohydrate 74.3g; Fibre 7.6g

Smoked Trout Cannelloni

The smoked trout filling gives this cannelloni dish a deliciously different taste.

Serves 4–6

1 large onion, finely chopped
1 garlic clove, crushed
60ml/4 tbsp vegetable stock
2 x 400g/14oz cans chopped
   Italian plum tomatoes
2.5ml/½ tsp dried mixed herbs
1 smoked trout, about
   400g/14oz, or 225g/8oz fillets
75g/3oz/¾ cup frozen
   peas, thawed

75g/3oz/1½ cups
   fresh breadcrumbs
16 cannelloni tubes
salt and ground black pepper
25ml/1½ tbsp freshly grated
   Parmesan cheese

For the cheese sauce

25g/1oz/2 tbsp butter
25g/1oz/¼ cup plain
   (all-purpose) flour
350ml/12fl oz/1½ cups
   skimmed milk
freshly grated nutmeg

1 Simmer the onion, garlic and stock in a large covered pan for 3 minutes. Uncover and continue to cook, stirring the mixture occasionally, until the stock has reduced entirely.

2 Stir the tomatoes and herbs into the onion mixture. Simmer, uncovered, for a further 10 minutes, until very thick.

3 Meanwhile, skin the smoked trout. Carefully flake the flesh and discard the bones. Mix the fish together with the tomato mixture, peas, breadcrumbs, salt and ground black pepper.

4 Preheat the oven to 190°C/375°F/Gas 5. Spoon the filling into the cannelloni tubes and arrange them side by side in a lightly greased ovenproof dish.

5 To make the sauce, melt the butter in a pan, add the flour and cook for 2–3 minutes, whisking constantly. Pour in the milk and bring to the boil, whisking, until the sauce thickens. Simmer for 2–3 minutes, stirring. Season with salt, pepper and nutmeg.

6 Pour the sauce over the cannelloni and sprinkle with the Parmesan. Bake in the oven for 35–40 minutes, until golden.

Energy 410Kcal/1735kJ; Fat 9.3g; Saturated Fat 2.1g; Carbohydrate 62.3g; Fibre 4.5g

Tuna Lasagne

Two popular Italian ingredients, tuna and pasta, combine to make a tasty lasagne that is sure to be a big hit with all the family.

Serves 6

12–16 fresh or dried
   lasagne sheets
15g/½oz butter
1 small onion, finely chopped
1 garlic clove, finely chopped
115g/4oz mushrooms,
   thinly sliced
60ml/4 tbsp dry white wine
   (optional)

600ml/1 pint/2½ cups white
   sauce (see page 59)
150ml/¼ pint/⅔ cup
   whipping cream
45ml/3 tbsp chopped
   fresh parsley
2 x 200g/7oz cans tuna, drained
2 canned pimientos, cut into strips
65g/2½oz/generous ½ cup
   frozen peas, thawed
115g/4oz mozzarella
   cheese, grated
30ml/2 tbsp freshly grated
   Parmesan cheese
salt and ground black pepper

1 For fresh lasagne, cook in a pan of salted boiling water until *al dente*. For dried, soak in a bowl of hot water for 3–5 minutes. Place the lasagne in a colander and rinse with cold water. Lay on a dish towel to drain.

2 Preheat the oven to 180°C/350°F/Gas 4. Melt the butter in a pan and cook the onion until soft.

3 Add the garlic and mushrooms to the pan and cook until soft, stirring occasionally. Pour in the wine, if using. Boil for 1 minute, then stir in the white sauce, cream and parsley. Season.

4 Spoon a thin layer of sauce over the base of a 30 x 23cm/ 12 x 9in baking dish. Cover with a layer of lasagne sheets.

5 Flake the tuna. Scatter half the tuna, pimiento strips, peas and mozzarella over the lasagne. Spoon one-third of the remaining sauce over the top and cover with another layer of lasagne.

6 Repeat the layers, ending with pasta and sauce. Sprinkle with the Parmesan. Bake for 30–40 minutes, or until lightly browned.

Energy 653Kcal/2744kJ; Fat 27.7g; Saturated Fat 14g; Carbohydrate 69.1g; Fibre 3.2g

Cannelloni with Tuna

Children love this pasta dish. Fontina cheese has a sweet, nutty flavour and very good melting qualities. Look for it in large supermarkets and Italian delicatessens.

Serves 4–6
50g/2oz/¼ cup butter
50g/2oz/½ cup plain
   (all-purpose) flour
about 900ml/1½ pints/3¾ cups
   hot milk
2 x 200g/7oz cans tuna, drained
115g/4oz/1 cup grated
   Fontina cheese
1.5ml/¼ tsp grated nutmeg
12 no pre-cook cannelloni tubes
50g/2oz/⅔ cup freshly grated
   Parmesan cheese
salt and ground black pepper
fresh herbs, to garnish

1 Melt the butter in a heavy pan, add the flour and stir over low heat for 1–2 minutes. Remove the pan from the heat and gradually add 350 ml/12 fl oz/1½ cups of the milk, beating vigorously after each addition. Return the pan to the heat and whisk for 1–2 minutes, until the sauce is very thick and smooth. Remove from the heat.

2 Mix the drained tuna with about 120 ml/4 fl oz/½ cup of the warm white sauce in a bowl. Add salt and black pepper to taste. Preheat the oven to 180°C/350°F/Gas 4.

3 Gradually whisk the remaining milk into the rest of the sauce, return to the heat and simmer, whisking, until thickened. Add the grated Fontina and nutmeg, and season with salt and pepper to taste. Simmer for a few minutes, stirring frequently. Pour one-third of the sauce into a baking dish.

4 Fill the cannelloni tubes with the tuna mixture, pushing it in with the handle of a teaspoon. Place the cannelloni in a single layer in the dish. Thin the remaining sauce with a little more milk if necessary, then pour it over the cannelloni.

5 Sprinkle the sauce with freshly grated Parmesan cheese and bake for 30 minutes, or until the top is golden. Serve immediately, garnished with herbs.

Energy 502Kcal/2110kJ; Fat 22.7g; Saturated Fat 11.4g; Carbohydrate 44.3g; Fibre 1.7g

Shellfish Lasagne

This is a luxury lasagne with a superb flavour.

Serves 4–6
4–6 fresh scallops, shelled
450g/1lb raw large peeled
   prawns (shrimp)
1 garlic clove, crushed
75g/3oz/6 tbsp butter
50g/2oz/½ cup plain
   (all-purpose) flour
600ml/1 pint/2½ cups hot milk
100ml/3½fl oz/scant ½ cup
   double (heavy) cream
100ml/3½fl oz/scant ½ cup dry
   white wine
2 sachets saffron powder
good pinch of cayenne pepper
130g/4½oz Fontina cheese,
   thinly sliced
75g/3oz/1 cup freshly grated
   Parmesan cheese
6–8 fresh lasagne sheets,
   pre-cooked if necessary
salt and ground black pepper

1 Preheat the oven to 190°C/375°F/Gas 5. Cut the scallops, their corals and the prawns into bite-size pieces and spread in a dish. Sprinkle with the garlic and salt and pepper to taste. Melt a third of the butter in a medium pan, add the scallops, corals and prawns and toss over medium heat for 1–2 minutes, or just until the prawns turn pink. Remove with a slotted spoon.

2 Add the remaining butter to the pan and melt over low heat. Sprinkle in the flour and cook, stirring, for 1–2 minutes, then increase the heat to medium and add the hot milk a little at a time, whisking vigorously after each addition. Bring to the boil and cook, stirring, until the sauce is smooth and very thick. Whisk in the cream, wine, saffron powder, cayenne and salt and pepper to taste, then remove the sauce from the heat.

3 Spread about a third of the sauce in a baking dish. Arrange half the Fontina slices over the sauce and sprinkle with about a third of the grated Parmesan. Scatter about half the shellfish evenly on top, then cover with half the lasagne sheets. Repeat the layers, then cover with the remaining sauce and Parmesan.

4 Bake the lasagne for 30–40 minutes, or until golden brown and bubbling. Allow to stand for 10 minutes before serving.

Energy 638Kcal/2670kJ; Fat 34g; Saturated Fat 20.8g; Carbohydrate 38.1g; Fibre 1.2g

Lasagne with Three Cheeses

This full-flavoured and hearty lasagne was invented in the United States by Italian immigrants who made good use of all the ingredients available to them.

Serves 6–8
25g/1oz/2 tbsp butter
15ml/1 tbsp olive oil
225–250g/8–9oz/2–2¼ cups button (white) mushrooms, quartered
30ml/2 tbsp chopped fresh flat leaf parsley

450g/1lb jar Bolognese sauce
250–350ml/8–12fl oz/1–1½ cups hot beef stock

9–12 fresh lasagne sheets, pre-cooked if necessary
450g/1lb/2 cups ricotta cheese
1 large (US extra large) egg
3 x 130g/4½oz packets mozzarella cheese, drained and thinly sliced
115g/4oz/1¼ cups freshly grated Parmesan cheese
salt and ground black pepper

1 Preheat the oven to 190°C/375°F/Gas 5. Melt the butter in the oil in a frying pan. Add the mushrooms, with salt and pepper to taste, and toss over medium to high heat for 5–8 minutes, until the mushrooms are tender and quite dry. Remove the pan from the heat and stir in the parsley.

2 Heat the Bolognese Sauce and stir in enough hot beef stock to make the sauce quite runny. Stir in the mushroom and parsley mixture, then spread about a quarter of this sauce over the bottom of a baking dish. Cover with 3–4 sheets of lasagne.

3 Beat together the ricotta and egg in a bowl, with salt and pepper to taste, then spread about a third of the mixture over the lasagne sheets. Cover with a third of the mozzarella slices, then sprinkle with about a quarter of the grated Parmesan.

4 Repeat these layers twice, using half the remaining meat sauce each time, and finishing with the remaining Parmesan.

5 Bake the lasagne for 30–40 minutes, or until the cheese topping is golden brown and bubbling. Allow to stand for about 10 minutes before serving.

Energy 533Kcal/2226kJ; Fat 32.4g; Saturated Fat 18.7g; Carbohydrate 29.7g; Fibre 1.4g

Lasagne with Lamb

Layered with lamb rather than beef, this is a different take on the classic lasagne.

Serves 4–6
15ml/1 tbsp olive oil
1 small onion, finely chopped
450g/1lb/2 cups minced (ground) lamb
1 garlic clove, crushed
45ml/3 tbsp dry white wine
5ml/1 tsp dried mixed herbs
450ml/¾ pint/2 cups passata (bottled, strained tomatoes)

12–16 fresh lasagne sheets, pre-cooked if necessary
30ml/2 tbsp freshly grated Parmesan cheese
salt and ground black pepper

For the white sauce
50g/2oz/¼ cup butter
50g/2oz/½ cup flour
900ml/1½ pints/3¾ cups hot milk
30ml/2 tbsp freshly grated Parmesan cheese
freshly grated nutmeg

1 Heat the oil in a pan and gently cook the onion for about 5 minutes, until softened. Add the minced lamb and garlic and cook gently for 10 minutes, stirring frequently. Stir in salt and pepper to taste, then add the wine and cook rapidly for about 2 minutes, stirring constantly. Stir in the herbs and passata. Simmer gently for 45 minutes to 1 hour, stirring occasionally.

2 Preheat the oven to 190°C/375°F/Gas 5. To make the white sauce, melt the butter in a pan, add the flour and cook, stirring, for 1–2 minutes. Add the milk a little at a time, whisking vigorously after each addition. Bring to the boil and cook, stirring, until the sauce is smooth and thick. Add the Parmesan, grate in fresh nutmeg to taste, season with a little salt and pepper and whisk well. Remove the pan from the heat.

3 Spread a few spoonfuls of meat sauce over the bottom of a baking dish and cover with three or four sheets of lasagne. Spread a quarter of the remaining meat sauce over the lasagne, then a quarter of the white sauce. Repeat the layers three times, finishing with white sauce.

4 Sprinkle the Parmesan over the surface and bake for 30–40 minutes, or until the topping is golden brown and bubbling.

Energy 587Kcal/2468kJ; Fat 25.7g; Saturated Fat 13g; Carbohydrate 59.9g; Fibre 2.5g

Lasagne with Meatballs

In southern Italy, where this type of lasagne is popular, salami and cheese are often added to the layers.

Serves 6–8
300g/11oz/1½ cups minced (ground) beef
300g/11oz/1½ cups minced (ground) pork
1 large (US extra large) egg
50g/2oz/1 cup fresh breadcrumbs
75ml/5 tbsp freshly grated Parmesan cheese
30ml/2 tbsp chopped fresh parsley
2 garlic cloves, crushed
60ml/4 tbsp olive oil
1 onion, finely chopped
1 carrot, finely chopped
1 celery stick, finely chopped
2 x 400g/14oz cans chopped Italian plum tomatoes
10ml/2 tsp dried oregano or basil
8–10 fresh lasagne sheets, pre-cooked if necessary
750ml/1¼ pints/3 cups white sauce (see page 59)
salt and ground black pepper

1 First make the meatballs. Put 175g/6oz/3¾ cup each of the minced beef and pork in a large bowl. Add the egg, bread-crumbs, 30ml/2 tbsp of the grated Parmesan, half the parsley and garlic and salt and pepper. Mix together, then squeeze and knead the mixture to bind. With cold hands roll into 60 very small balls. Place on a tray and chill for about 30 minutes.

2 To make the meat sauce, heat half the oil in a frying pan, add the onion, carrot, celery and remaining garlic and stir over low heat for 5 minutes, until softened. Add the remaining minced beef and pork and cook gently for 10 minutes. Season, then add the tomatoes, remaining parsley and the oregano. Cover and simmer gently for 45 minutes to 1 hour. Meanwhile, heat the remaining oil in a large, non-stick frying pan and cook the meatballs for 5–8 minutes, until brown. As they cook, transfer the meatballs to kitchen paper to drain.

3 Preheat the oven to 190°C/375°F/Gas 5. Spread one-third of the meat sauce in a large baking dish. Add half the meatballs, spread with a third of the béchamel and cover with half the lasagne. Repeat these layers, then top with the remaining béchamel. Sprinkle Parmesan on top. Bake for 30–40 minutes.

Energy 553Kcal/2320kJ; Fat 27g; Saturated Fat 11.3g; Carbohydrate 51g; Fibre 3g

Mixed Meat Cannelloni

Combining beef, pork and chicken for the filling makes this a rich and succulent cannelloni dish.

Serves 4
60ml/4 tbsp olive oil
1 onion, finely chopped
1 carrot, finely chopped
2 garlic cloves, crushed
2 ripe Italian plum tomatoes, peeled and finely chopped
130g/4½oz/½ cup minced (ground) beef
130g/4½oz/½ cup minced (ground) pork
250g/9oz minced (ground) chicken
30ml/2 tbsp brandy
25g/1oz/2 tbsp butter
90ml/6 tbsp panna da cucina or double (heavy) cream
16 dried cannelloni tubes
75g/3oz/1 cup freshly grated Parmesan cheese
salt and ground black pepper

For the white sauce
50g/2oz/¼ cup butter
50g/2oz/½ cup plain (all-purpose) flour
900ml/1½ pints/3¾ cups milk
freshly grated nutmeg

1 Heat the oil in a medium frying pan, add the onion, carrot, garlic and tomatoes and cook over low heat, stirring, for about 10 minutes, or until very soft.

2 Add all the minced meats to the pan and cook gently for about 10 minutes, stirring frequently to break up any lumps. Add the brandy, increase the heat and stir until it has reduced, then add the butter and cream and cook gently, stirring occasionally, for about 10 minutes. Allow to cool.

3 Preheat the oven to 190°C/375°F/Gas 5. To make the white sauce, melt the butter in a medium pan, add the flour and cook, stirring, for 1–2 minutes. Gradually whisk in the milk, bring to the boil and cook, stirring, until the sauce is smooth and thick. Add nutmeg, salt and pepper to taste. Remove from the heat.

4 Spoon a little of the white sauce into a baking dish. Carefully fill the cannelloni tubes with the meat mixture and place in a single layer in the dish. Pour the remaining white sauce over the tubes, then sprinkle with Parmesan. Bake for 35–40 minutes.

Energy 1025Kcal/4284kJ; Fat 59g; Saturated Fat 28.9g; Carbohydrate 71.3g; Fibre 3.4g

Cheese & Prosciutto Ravioli

Typical of southern Italian cuisine, these tasty ravioli are layered with tomato sauce.

Serves 4–6
1 quantity handmade Egg Pasta
    (see page 6)
flour, for dusting
60ml/4 tbsp freshly grated
    Pecorino cheese

For the filling
175g/6oz/³⁄₄ cup ricotta cheese
30ml/2 tbsp freshly grated
    Parmesan cheese

115g/4oz prosciutto, finely chopped
150g/5oz mozzarella cheese,
    drained and finely chopped
1 small egg
15ml/1 tbsp chopped fresh parsley

For the tomato sauce
30ml/2 tbsp olive oil
1 onion, finely chopped
400g/14oz can chopped Italian
    plum tomatoes
15ml/1 tbsp sun-dried tomato
    purée (paste)
5–10ml/1–2 tsp dried oregano
salt and ground black pepper

1 To make the sauce, heat the oil in a medium pan, add the onion and cook gently, stirring, for about 5 minutes, until soft. Add the tomatoes. Fill the empty can with water, pour into the pan, then stir in the tomato paste, oregano and salt and pepper to taste. Bring to the boil, cover the pan and simmer gently for 30 minutes, stirring occasionally. Add more water if necessary. Meanwhile, put all the filling ingredients in a bowl with salt and pepper to taste. Mix well with a fork.

2 Using a pasta machine, roll out one-quarter of the pasta into a 90cm–1m/36in–3ft strip. Cut into two 45–50cm/18–20in lengths. Using 2 teaspoons, put 10–12 little mounds of the filling evenly along one side of one of the pasta strips. Brush water around each mound, then fold the plain side of the pasta strip over the filling. Starting from the folded edge, press down gently around each mound, pushing the air out.

3 Sprinkle with flour. With a fluted pasta wheel, cut into small square shapes. Put the ravioli on floured dish towels. Repeat with the remaining pasta to make 80–96 ravioli. Cook in a large pan of boiling water for 4–5 minutes, until tender. Drain the ravioli and layer in a bowl with Pecorino and tomato sauce.

Ravioli with Pork & Turkey

These Roman-style meat ravioli are delightfully scented with fresh herbs.

Serves 8
1 quantity handmade Egg Pasta
    (see page 6)
50g/2oz/¹⁄₄ cup butter
flour, for dusting
1 bunch sage, leaves chopped
60ml/4 tbsp freshly grated
    Parmesan cheese

For the filling
25g/1oz/2 tbsp butter

150g/5oz/generous ¹⁄₂ cup
    minced (ground) pork
115g/4oz/¹⁄₂ cup minced
    (ground) turkey
4 fresh sage leaves, chopped
1 fresh sprig rosemary, leaves
    removed and finely chopped
30ml/2 tbsp dry white wine
65g/2¹⁄₂oz/¹⁄₄ cup ricotta cheese
45ml/3 tbsp freshly grated
    Parmesan cheese
1 egg, lightly beaten
freshly grated nutmeg
salt and ground black pepper

1 To make the filling, melt the butter in a pan, add the pork and turkey and the herbs and cook for 5–6 minutes. Season and stir. Add the wine and simmer for 1–2 minutes, until reduced slightly. Cover and simmer gently for about 20 minutes. With a slotted spoon, transfer the meat to a bowl; cool.

2 Add the cheeses to the bowl with the egg and freshly grated nutmeg to taste. Stir well to mix the ingredients thoroughly.

3 Using a pasta machine, roll out one-quarter of the pasta into a 90cm–1m/35in–3ft strip. Cut into two 45–50cm/18–20in lengths. Using a teaspoon, put 10–12 little mounds of the filling evenly along one side of one of the pasta strips. Brush water around each mound, then fold the plain side of the pasta strip over the filling. Starting from the folded edge, press down around each mound, pushing the air out. Dust with flour.

4 With a pasta wheel, cut into square shapes. Dust with flour. Put the ravioli on floured dish towels. Repeat with the rest of the pasta to make 80–96 ravioli. Cook in boiling water for 4–5 minutes. Meanwhile, heat the sage in the butter until sizzling. Drain the ravioli and serve with the sage butter and Parmesan.

Energy 393Kcal/1653kJ; Fat 17.1g; Saturated Fat 9.4g; Carbohydrate 42g; Fibre 1.6g

Energy 521Kcal/2194kJ; Fat 21g; Saturated Fat 10.4g; Carbohydrate 59.5g; Fibre 3g

Turkey Pasta Bake

Layers of turkey and macaroni topped with a light white sauce make up this healthy pasta bake.

Serves 4–6

450g/1lb/2 cups lean minced (ground) turkey
1 large onion, finely chopped
60ml/4 tbsp tomato purée (paste)
250ml/8fl oz/1 cup red wine or stock
5ml/1 tsp ground cinnamon
300g/11oz/2¾ cups dried macaroni
25g/1oz/2 tbsp sunflower margarine
25g/1oz/3 tbsp plain (all-purpose) flour
300ml/½ pint/1¼ cups skimmed milk
5ml/1 tsp grated nutmeg
2 tomatoes, sliced
60ml/4 tbsp wholemeal breadcrumbs
salt and ground black pepper
green salad, to serve

1 Preheat the oven to 220°C/425°F/Gas 7. Fry the turkey and onion in a non-stick pan without any fat, stirring until lightly browned and the turkey fat has reduced.

2 Stir in the tomato purée, red wine or stock and cinnamon. Season with salt and pepper to taste, then cover and simmer for about 5 minutes.

3 Bring a pan of lightly salted water to the boil, add the pasta and cook until al dente. Drain the pasta.

4 Layer the macaroni with the turkey mixture in a wide ovenproof dish.

5 Melt the margarine in a pan and add the flour, stirring. Cook for 2–3 minutes, stirring constantly, then gradually add the milk and whisk over medium heat, until thickened and smooth.

6 Whisk the nutmeg and salt and pepper to taste into the sauce, then pour evenly over the pasta. Arrange the tomato slices on top and sprinkle with lines of breadcrumbs.

7 Bake in the oven for 30–35 minutes, or until golden brown.

Energy 397Kcal/1683kJ; Fat 7.2g; Saturated Fat 1.2g; Carbohydrate 53.3g; Fibre 2.5g

Rotolo di Pasta

A giant roll of pasta with a spinach filling, which is poached, sliced and baked with béchamel sauce. This recipe is made the traditional way with sheets of fresh egg pasta.

Serves 6

700g/1½lb frozen chopped spinach, thawed
50g/2oz/¼ cup butter
1 onion, chopped
100g/4oz ham or bacon, diced
225g/8oz/1 cup ricotta or curd (farmer's) cheese
1 egg
freshly grated nutmeg
6 fresh spinach lasagne sheets
1.2 litres/2 pints/5 cups béchamel sauce, warmed (see page 54)
50g/2oz/⅔ cup freshly grated Parmesan cheese
salt and ground black pepper

1 Squeeze the excess moisture from the spinach and set aside. Melt the butter in a saucepan and fry the onion until golden. Add the ham and fry until beginning to brown. Take off the heat and stir in the spinach. Cool slightly, then beat in the ricotta or curd cheese and the egg. Season with salt, pepper and nutmeg.

2 Roll the pasta out to a rectangle about 30 × 40cm/12 × 16in. Spread the filling all over, leaving a 1cm/½in border all round the edge of the rectangle.

3 Roll up the pasta and filling from the shorter end and wrap in muslin to form a sausage shape, tying the ends with string.

4 Poach the pasta roll in a very large pan (or fish kettle) of simmering water for about 20 minutes, or until firm. Carefully remove, drain and then unwrap. Leave to cool.

5 When you are ready to finish the dish, preheat the oven to 200°C/400°F/Gas 6. Cut the pasta roll into 2.5cm/1in slices. Spoon a little béchamel sauce over the base of a shallow baking dish and arrange the slices on top, slightly overlapping.

6 Spoon the remaining sauce over the roll slices, sprinkle with cheese and bake for 15–20 minutes, or until browned. Allow to stand for a few minutes before serving.

Energy 703Kcal/2932kJ; Fat 38.9g; Saturated Fat 18g; Carbohydrate 62.3g; Fibre 4.4g

Chicken Lasagne

A variation of the traditional beef lasagne, this is an excellent dish for all-round entertaining. Serve simply with a green salad.

Serves 8
30ml/2 tbsp olive oil
900g/2lb/4 cups minced (ground)
  raw chicken
225g/8oz rindless streaky (fatty)
  bacon rashers (strips), chopped
2 garlic cloves, crushed
450g/1lb leeks, sliced
225g/8oz carrots, diced
30ml/2 tbsp tomato
  purée (paste)

450ml/³/₄ pint/1³/₄ cups
  chicken stock
12 no pre-cook dried
  lasagne sheets

For the cheese sauce
50g/2oz/¹/₄ cup butter
50g/2oz/¹/₂ cup plain
  (all-purpose) flour
600ml/1 pint/2¹/₂ cups milk
115g/4oz/1 cup grated mature
  Cheddar cheese
1.5ml/¹/₄ tsp English
  mustard powder
salt and ground black pepper

1 Heat the oil in a large flameproof casserole and brown the minced chicken and bacon briskly, separating the pieces with a wooden spoon. Add the crushed garlic cloves, chopped leeks and diced carrots and cook for about 5 minutes, until softened. Add the tomato purée, stock and seasoning. Bring to the boil, cover and simmer for 30 minutes.

2 To make the sauce, melt the butter in a pan, add the flour and gradually blend in the milk, stirring until smooth. Bring to the boil, stirring all the time until thickened, and simmer for several minutes. Add half the grated Cheddar cheese and the mustard and season to taste.

3 Preheat the oven to 190°C/375°F/Gas 5. Layer the chicken mixture, lasagne and half the cheese sauce in a 2.5 litre/ 4 pints/10½ cups ovenproof dish, starting and finishing with the chicken mixture.

4 Pour the remaining cheese sauce over, sprinkle with the remaining cheese and bake for 1 hour, or until lightly browned.

Energy 558Kcal/2347kJ; Fat 23g; Saturated Fat 10.4g; Carbohydrate 45.2g; Fibre 3.5g

Chicken Cannelloni al Forno

A lighter alternative to the usual beef-filled, béchamel-coated version. Try filling with ricotta cheese, onion and mushroom for a vegetarian dish.

Serves 4–6
450g/1lb chicken breast
  fillets, cooked
225g/8oz mushrooms
2 garlic cloves, crushed
30ml/2 tbsp chopped fresh
  parsley
15ml/1 tbsp chopped tarragon

1 egg, beaten
freshly squeezed lemon juice
12–18 fresh or dried
  cannelloni tubes
450g/1lb jar Bolognese sauce
50g/2oz/²/₃ cup grated
  Parmesan cheese
salt and freshly ground black
  pepper
fresh parsley sprig, to garnish

1 Preheat the oven to 200°C/400°F/Gas 6. Place the chicken in a blender or food processor and process until finely minced (ground). Transfer to a bowl.

2 Place the mushrooms, garlic, parsley and tarragon in the blender or food processor and process until finely minced.

3 Beat the mushroom mixture into the chicken with the egg, salt and ground black pepper and lemon juice to taste.

4 Bring a large pan of lightly salted water to the boil, add the cannelloni tubes and cook until al dente. Drain well and pat dry on a clean dish towel.

5 Place the filling in a piping bag fitted with a large plain nozzle. Use to fill each tube of cannelloni.

6 Lay the filled cannelloni tightly together in a single layer in a buttered shallow ovenproof dish. Spoon the Tomato Sauce over and sprinkle with Parmesan cheese. Bake in the oven for 30 minutes or until brown and bubbling. Serve the cannelloni garnished with a sprig of parsley.

Energy 458Kcal/1938kJ; Fat 10.1g; Saturated Fat 3.7g; Carbohydrate 62.2g; Fibre 3.6g

Basic Pizza Dough

Pizzas originate from the south of Italy and have developed into a universally-loved family meal. Making fresh dough takes a little practice but gives a really tasty pizza base.

Serves 4 as a main course or 8 as an appetizer

25g/1oz/2½ tbsp fresh bread yeast or 15g/½oz/1½ tbsp active dried yeast
250ml/8fl oz/1 cup lukewarm water
pinch of sugar
5ml/1 tsp salt
350–400g/12-14oz/3–3½ cups unbleached strong white bread flour

1 Warm a medium mixing bowl by swirling some hot water in it. Drain. Place the yeast in the bowl, and pour on the warm water. Stir in the sugar, mix with a fork, and allow to stand until the yeast has dispersed and starts to foam, 5–10 minutes.

2 Mix in the salt and about one-third of the flour. Mix in another third of the flour, stirring until the dough forms a mass and begins to pull away from the sides of the bowl.

3 Sprinkle some of the remaining flour onto a smooth work surface. Remove the dough from the bowl and begin to knead it, working in the remaining flour a little at a time. Knead for 8–10 minutes. By the end the dough should be elastic and smooth. Form it into a ball.

4 Lightly oil a large mixing bowl. Place the dough in the bowl. Stretch a damp (not wet) dish towel across the top of the bowl, and leave itin a warm place, until the dough has doubled in volume, about 40–50 minutes or more, depending on the type of yeast used. (If you do not have a warm enough place, turn the oven on to medium heat for 10 minutes before you knead the dough. Turn it off. Place the bowl with the dough in the turned-off oven with the door closed and let it rise there.) To test whether the dough has risen enough, poke two fingers into it. If the indentations remain, the dough is ready.

5 Punch the dough to release the air. Knead for 1–2 minutes. Divide the dough, if you wish, to make 2–4 small pizzas.

6 Pat the ball of dough out into a flat circle on a lightly floured surface. With a rolling pin, roll it out to a thickness of about 5mm/¼in. If you are using a pizza pan, roll the dough out about 4mm/¼in larger than the size of the pan to allow for the rim.

7 Place the pizza base on a lightly oiled pan, folding the extra dough under to make a thicker rim around the edge. Place it on a lightly oiled baking tray (cookie sheet). The dough is now ready for topping.

Variation
Replace half the flour with wholemeal (whole-wheat) flour and add 30ml/2 tbsp olive oil if you want a healthier version.

Butternut Squash & Sage Pizza

The combination of the sweet butternut squash, pungent sage and sharp goat's cheese works wonderfully on this pizza.

Serves 2–3
1 quantity Basic Pizza Dough (see left)
15g/½ oz/1 tbsp butter
30ml/2 tbsp olive oil
1 shallot, finely chopped
1 small butternut squash, peeled, seeded and cubed
8 fresh sage leaves
350ml/12fl oz/1½ cups bottled Italian tomato sauce
75g/3oz mozzarella cheese, sliced
75g/3oz firm goat's cheese
salt and ground black pepper

1 Preheat the oven to 200°C/400°F/Gas 6. Roll out the dough on a lightly floured surface to a 25–30cm/10–12cm round and place on a baking sheet.

2 Melt the butter in the oil in a roasting pan. Add the shallot, squash and half the sage leaves. Toss well to coat all over in oil. Roast the vegetables for 15–20 minutes, until tender.

3 Increase the oven temperature to 220°C/425°F/Gas 7. Spread the Tomato Sauce evenly over the surface of the pizza, to within 1cm/½in of the edge.

4 Spoon the squash mixture evenly over the pizza, arrange the mozzarella on top and crumble over the goat's cheese.

5 Scatter the remaining sage leaves over the pizza and season with plenty of salt and pepper. Bake for 15–20 minutes, until the cheese has melted and the crust is golden. Serve immediately.

Cook's Tip
For a quick scone base, mix 225g/8oz/2 cups self-raising (self-rising) flour with a pinch of salt, then rub in 50g/2oz/¼ cup diced butter. Pour in about 150ml/¼ pint/⅔ cup milk and mix to a soft dough. Pat out to a 25cm/10in round, top as suggested above and bake for about 20 minutes.

Energy 674Kcal/2828kJ; Fat 34.6g; Saturated Fat 13.9g; Carbohydrate 73.8g; Fibre 6g

New Potato, Rosemary & Garlic Pizza

New potatoes, smoked mozzarella, rosemary and garlic make the flavour of this pizza unique.

Serves 2–3
1 quantity Basic Pizza Dough (see page 64)
flour, for dusting

350g/12oz new potatoes
45ml/3 tbsp olive oil
2 garlic cloves, crushed
1 red onion, very thinly sliced
150g/5oz/1¼ cups grated smoked mozzarella cheese
10ml/2 tsp chopped rosemary
salt and ground black pepper
30ml/2 tbsp freshly grated Parmesan cheese, to serve

1 Preheat the oven to 220°C/425°F/Gas 7. Roll out the dough on a lightly floured surface to a 25–30cm/10–12cm round and place on a baking sheet.

2 Bring a large pan of lightly salted water to the boil and cook the potatoes for 5 minutes. Drain well. When cool, peel the potatoes and slice them thinly.

3 Heat 30ml/2 tbsp of the oil in a frying pan. Add the sliced potatoes and garlic and fry over medium heat, stirring occasionally, for 5–8 minutes, until tender.

4 Brush the pizza base with the remaining oil. Scatter over the onion, then arrange the potatoes on top. Sprinkle over the mozzarella and rosemary. Grind over plenty of black pepper. Bake for 15–20 minutes, until the crust is crisp and golden. Sprinkle over the grated Parmesan and serve.

Cook's Tips
• Next time you find yourself with leftover new potatoes, use them to make this tasty pizza.
• Smoked mozzarella, also known as mozzarella affumicata, is available from supermarkets and delicatessens.

Fiorentina Pizza

An egg adds the finishing touch to this spinach pizza; it's best when the yolk is still slightly soft.

Serves 3–4
1 quantity Basic Pizza Dough (see page 64)
flour, for dusting
45ml/3 tbsp olive oil

1 small red onion, thinly sliced
175g/6oz fresh spinach, stalks removed
350ml/12fl oz/1½ cups bottled tomato pasta sauce
freshly grated nutmeg
150g/5oz mozzarella cheese
1 egg
25g/1oz/¼ cup grated Gruyère cheese

1 Roll out the dough on a lightly floured surface to a 25–30cm/10–12cm round and place on a baking sheet.

2 Heat 15ml/1 tbsp of the olive oil. Add the onion and fry over a low heat, stirring occasionally, for 5 minutes, until soft. Add the spinach and fry until wilted. Drain any excess liquid.

3 Preheat the oven to 220°C/425°F/Gas 7. Brush the pizza base with half the remaining olive oil. Spread the Tomato Sauce evenly over the base, using the back of a spoon, to within 1cm/½in of the edge. Then cover the top of the pizza with the spinach mixture. Sprinkle over a little freshly grated nutmeg.

4 Slice the mozzarella thinly and arrange it over the spinach. Drizzle over the remaining oil. Bake for 10 minutes, then remove from the oven.

5 Make a small well in the centre of the pizza topping and carefully break the egg into the hole. Sprinkle over the Gruyère. Return the pizza to the oven for 5–10 minutes, until crisp and golden. Serve immediately.

Variation
For an instant meal, buy a ready-prepared pizza base and use a bottled tomato pasta sauce, flavoured with basil.

Energy 689Kcal/2886kJ; Fat 37g; Saturated Fat 12.8g; Carbohydrate 67.9g; Fibre 4.9g

Energy 690Kcal/2899kJ; Fat 30.1g; Saturated Fat 10.6g; Carbohydrate 85.2g; Fibre 4.2g

Spring Vegetable & Pine Nut Pizza

With its colourful topping of tender young vegetables, the pizza makes a lovely, fresh tasting meal.

Serves 2–3
1 quantity Basic Pizza Dough (see page 64)
flour, for dusting
45ml/3 tbsp olive oil
1 garlic clove, crushed
4 spring onions (scallions), sliced
2 courgettes (zucchini), sliced
1 leek, thinly sliced
115g/4oz asparagus tips, sliced
15ml/1 tbsp chopped fresh oregano

30ml/2 tbsp pine nuts
50g/2oz/1/2 cup grated mozzarella cheese
30ml/2 tbsp freshly grated Parmesan cheese
salt and ground black pepper

For the tomato sauce
15ml/1 tbsp olive oil
1 onion, finely chopped
1 garlic clove, crushed
400ml/14oz can chopped Italian plum tomatoes
15ml/1 tbsp tomato purée (paste)
15ml/1 tbsp chopped fresh herbs
pinch of sugar

1 To make the tomato sauce, heat the oil in a pan and fry the onion and garlic over low heat, stirring occasionally, for about 5 minutes, until softened but not browned. Add the remaining ingredients, stir well and simmer for 15–20 minutes, until the mixture is thick and flavoursome.

2 Preheat the oven to 220°C/425°F/Gas 7. Roll out the dough on a lightly floured surface to a 25–30cm/10–12cm round and place on a baking sheet. Brush the pizza base with 15ml/1 tbsp of the olive oil, then spread the tomato sauce evenly over the top to within 1cm/1/2in of the edge.

3 Heat half the remaining olive oil in a frying pan and fry the garlic, spring onions, courgettes, leek and asparagus, stirring over medium heat for 3–5 minutes.

4 Arrange the vegetables over the tomato sauce, then sprinkle the oregano and pine nuts over the top. Mix the cheeses and sprinkle over. Drizzle with the remaining olive oil and season well. Bake for 15–20 minutes, until crisp and golden.

Roasted Vegetable & Goat's Cheese Pizza

This pizza incorporates the smoky flavours of roasted vegetables and the tangy taste of goat's cheese.

Serves 3
1 aubergine (eggplant), cut into thick chunks
2 courgettes (zucchini), sliced lengthways
1 red (bell) pepper, quartered and seeded

1 yellow (bell) pepper, quartered and seeded
1 small red onion, cut into wedges
90ml/6 tbsp olive oil
1 quantity Basic Pizza Dough (see page 64)
400g/14oz can chopped Italian plum tomatoes, well drained
115g/4oz goat's cheese, cubed
15ml/1 tbsp chopped fresh thyme
ground black pepper
green olive paste, to serve

1 Preheat the oven to 220°C/425°F/Gas 7. Place the vegetables in a roasting pan. Brush with 60ml/4 tbsp of the oil. Roast for 30 minutes, until charred, turning the peppers once. Remove the vegetables but leave the oven on. Put the peppers in a bowl and cover with crumpled kitchen paper. When cool enough to handle, peel off the skins and cut the flesh into thick strips.

2 Roll out the dough on a lightly floured surface to a 25–30cm/10–12cm round. Brush the base with half the remaining oil and spread over the drained tomatoes. Arrange the vegetables on top and dot with the goat's cheese. Scatter over the thyme.

3 Drizzle over the remaining oil and season. Bake for 15–20 minutes, until crisp. Spoon the olive paste over to serve.

> **Cook's Tip**
> *To make a tasty green olive paste, put 40 pitted green olives and 5ml/1 tsp capers in a food processor. Add four pieces of drained sun-dried tomatoes in oil, 5ml/1 tsp ground almonds, one chopped garlic clove and a pinch of ground cumin. Process briefly, add 60ml/4 tbsp olive oil and process to a paste.*

Energy 656Kcal/2745kJ; Fat 34.4g; Saturated Fat 7.2g; Carbohydrate 69g; Fibre 7.1g

Energy 421Kcal/1744kJ; Fat 33.6g; Saturated Fat 10.5g; Carbohydrate 17.6g; Fibre 6.4g

Wild Mushroom Pizzettes

With their delicate earthy flavour, wild mushrooms make a delicious topping for these little pizzas. Serve as an unusual starter or for a stylish light meal.

Serves 4
45ml/3 tbsp olive oil
350g/12oz/4½ cups fresh wild
    mushrooms, sliced
2 shallots, chopped
2 garlic cloves, finely chopped
30ml/2 tbsp chopped fresh mixed
    thyme and flat leaf parsley
1 quantity Basic Pizza Dough (see
    page 64)
flour, for dusting
40g/1½ oz/s ½ cup grated
    Gruyère cheese
30ml/2 tbsp freshly grated
    Parmesan cheese
salt and ground black pepper

1 Preheat the oven to 220°C/425°F/Gas 7. Heat 30ml/2 tbsp of the oil in a frying pan. Add the mushrooms, shallots and garlic and fry over medium heat, stirring occasionally, until all the juices have evaporated.

2 Stir in half the mixed herbs and season to taste with salt and pepper, then set aside to cool.

3 Divide the dough into four pieces and roll out each one on a lightly floured surface to a 13cm/5in circle. Place well apart on two greased baking sheets, then push up the dough edges on each to form a thin rim. Brush the bases with oil and top with the mushroom mixture, leaving a small rim all the way around.

4 Mix the Gruyère and Parmesan cheeses, then sprinkle one-quarter of the mixture over each of the pizzettes. Bake for 15–20 minutes, until crisp and golden. Remove from the oven and scatter over the remaining herbs to serve.

> **Cook's Tip**
> *Fresh wild mushrooms add a distinctive flavour to the topping, but a mixture of cultivated mushrooms, such as shiitake, oyster and chestnut mushrooms, would do just as well.*

Cheese & Pimiento Pizzettes

Great party food with lots of Italian style, these tempting mini pizzas take only minutes to make and will be eaten even quicker.

Makes 24
2 quantities Basic Pizza Dough
    (see page 64)
60ml/4 tbsp olive oil
30ml/2 tbsp olive paste
175g/6oz goat's cheese
1 large canned or bottled
    pimiento, drained
30ml/2 tbsp chopped fresh thyme
30ml/2 tbsp pine nuts
ground black pepper
fresh thyme sprigs, to garnish

1 Preheat the oven to 220°C/425°F/Gas 7. Divide the pizza dough into 24 pieces and roll out each one on a lightly floured surface to a small oval, about 3mm/⅛in thick.

2 Place well apart on greased baking sheets and prick all over with a fork. Brush with 30ml/2 tbsp of the oil.

3 Spread a thin layer of the olive paste on each oval and crumble over the feta. Cut the pimiento into thin strips and pile on top of the cheese.

4 Sprinkle each pizzette with thyme and pine nuts. Drizzle over the remaining oil and grind over plenty of black pepper. Bake for 10–15 minutes, until crisp and golden. Garnish with thyme sprigs and serve immediately.

> **Cook's Tip**
> *Use a goat's cheese with a firm texture, suitable for crumbling.*

> **Variations**
> • *Feta makes an interesting change to goat's cheese.*
> • *Either black or green olive paste can be used for this recipe. Tapenade is also widely available from supermarkets and delicatessens and makes a good substitute.*

Energy 384Kcal/1611kJ; Fat 18g; Saturated Fat 5g; Carbohydrate 44.7g; Fibre 2.8g

Energy 117Kcal/491kJ; Fat 5.5g; Saturated Fat 1.3g; Carbohydrate 14.5g; Fibre 0.6g

Calzone

A calzone is like a folded pizza, with the dough wrapped around a cheese and vegetable filling. Here the traditional tomato and garlic filling is enlivened with chunks of sweet melting cheese, olives and sliced peppery sausage.

Makes 4
30ml/2 tbsp extra virgin olive oil
1 small red onion, thinly sliced
2 garlic cloves, crushed
400g/14oz can chopped Italian
   plum tomatoes
50g/2oz sliced pepperoni or
   chorizo sausage
50g/2oz/1/2 cup pitted
   black olives
1 quantity Basic Pizza Dough
   (see page 64)
flour, for dusting
200g/7oz mozzarella or other
   semi-soft cheese, diced
5ml/1 tsp dried oregano
salt and ground black pepper
oregano sprigs, to garnish

1 Heat the oil in a frying pan and fry the sliced onion and crushed garlic for 5 minutes. Add the chopped tomatoes and cook for a further 5 minutes, or until slightly reduced. Add the sliced pepperoni and pitted black olives. Season with plenty of salt and pepper.

2 Divide the dough into four portions. Roll out each portion on a lightly flour surface into a round measuring about 20cm/8in. Preheat the oven to 200°C/400°F/Gas 6. Lightly grease two baking sheets.

3 Spread the tomato filling on half of each dough circle, leaving a margin around the edge. Scatter the mozzarella cheese on top. Sprinkle the filling with the dried oregano.

4 Dampen the edges of the dough circle with cold water. Fold the dough in half and press the edges together with your fingers to seal securely.

5 Place two calzones on each baking sheet. Bake for 12–15 minutes, until the dough is risen and golden. Cool for 2 minutes, then loosen from the sheet with a palette knife and transfer to individual serving plates. Serve at once, garnished with oregano.

Energy 625Kcal/2626kJ; Fat 28.2g; Saturated Fat 9.8g; Carbohydrate 75g; Fibre 4g

Sun-dried Tomato Calzone

Hot things up with a few more red chilli flakes.

Serves 2
3 shallots, chopped
30ml/2 tbsp olive oil
4 baby aubergines
   (eggplants), cubed
1 garlic clove, chopped
50g/2oz/1/3 cup sun-dried
   tomatoes in oil, drained
1.5ml/1/4 tsp dried red chilli flakes
10ml/2 tsp chopped fresh thyme
75g/3oz mozzarella cheese
1/2 quantity Basic Pizza Dough
   (see page 64)
salt and ground black pepper
flour, for dusting

1 Preheat the oven to 220°C/425°F/Gas 7. Fry the shallots in oil until soft. Add the aubergines, garlic, tomatoes, chilli, thyme and seasoning. Cook for 5 minutes. Divide the dough in half and roll out each piece on a lightly floured surface to an 18cm/7in round.

2 Spread the aubergine mixture over half of each round, leaving a 2.5cm/1in border, then scatter the diced mozzarella on top. Dampen the edges with water, then fold over the dough to enclose the filling. Press the edges together. Place on greased baking sheets. Brush with oil and make a small hole in the top of each calzone. Bake for 15–20 minutes, until golden.

Margherita Pizza

This is a quick version of an ever-popular classic.

Serves 2
half a 300g/11oz packet pizza
   base mix
15ml/1 tbsp herb-infused olive oil
45ml/3 tbsp ready-made tomato
   and basil sauce
150g/5oz mozzarella, sliced
salt and ground black pepper

1 Make the pizza base mix following the packet instructions. Preheat the oven as instructed. Brush the base with a little of the oil and spread the tomato and basil sauce over the top.

2 Top with the mozzarella and bake for 25–30 minutes, or until golden. Drizzle with the remaining oil, season and serve.

Top Energy 732Kcal/3071kJ; Fat 32g; Saturated Fat 8.7g; Carbohydrate 97.4g; Fibre 7.8g
Above Energy 349Kcal/1466kJ; Fat 14.6g; Saturated Fat 6g; Carbohydrate 44g; Fibre 1.7g

Mushroom & Pesto Pizza

Capture all the wonderful flavours of home-baked Italian pizza with this recipe.

Serves 4
350g/12oz/3 cups strong white
   bread flour
1.5ml/¼ tsp salt
15g/½oz easy-blend (rapid-rise)
   dried yeast
15ml/1 tbsp olive oil
150ml/¼ pint warm water

For the topping
50g/2oz dried porcini mushrooms
25g/1oz/¾ cup fresh basil
25g/1oz/⅓ cup pine nuts
40g/1½oz Parmesan cheese,
   thinly sliced
105ml/7 tbsp olive oil
2 onions, thinly sliced
225g/8oz chestnut mushrooms,
   sliced
salt and ground black pepper

1 To make the pizza base, put the flour in a bowl with the salt, dried yeast and olive oil. Add 250ml/8fl oz/1 cup hand-hot water and mix to a dough using a round-bladed knife.

2 Turn on to a work surface and knead for 5 minutes until smooth. Place in a clean bowl, cover with clear film (plastic wrap) and leave in a warm place until doubled in bulk.

3 Meanwhile, make the topping. Soak the dried mushrooms in hot water for 20 minutes. Place the basil, pine nuts, Parmesan and 75ml/5 tbsp of the olive oil in a blender or food processor and process to make a smooth paste. Set the paste aside.

4 Fry the onions in the remaining olive oil for 3–4 minutes, until beginning to colour. Add the chestnut mushrooms and fry for 2 minutes. Stir in the drained porcini mushrooms and season lightly with salt and pepper.

5 Preheat the oven to 220°C/425°F/Gas 7. Lightly grease a large baking sheet. Turn the pizza dough on to a floured surface and roll out to a 30cm/12in round. Place on the baking sheet.

6 Spread the basil and pine nut mixture to within 1cm/½in of the edges. Spread the mushroom mixture on top. Bake the pizza for 35–40 minutes, until risen and golden.

Energy 631Kcal/2642kJ; Fat 31.3g; Saturated Fat 5.7g; Carbohydrate 76.6g; Fibre 5.3g

Ricotta & Fontina Pizzas

The combination of delicate mushrooms and a delicious creamy cheese makes a winning topping for pizza.

Serves 4
400g/14oz can chopped Italian
   plum tomatoes
150ml/¼ pint/⅔ cup passata
   (bottled, strained tomatoes)
5ml/1 tsp dried oregano
1 bay leaf
10ml/2 tsp malt vinegar
2 large garlic cloves, chopped
30ml/2 tbsp olive oil, plus extra

for brushing
350g/12oz/4 cups mixed
   mushrooms (chestnut, flat or
   button), sliced
1 quantity Basic Pizza Dough
   (see page 64)
flour, for dusting
30ml/2 tbsp chopped fresh
   oregano, plus whole leaves,
   to garnish
250g/9oz/generous 1 cup
   ricotta cheese
225g/8oz Fontina cheese, sliced
salt and ground black pepper

1 To make the topping, place the tomatoes, passata, herbs, vinegar and half of the garlic in a pan, cover and bring to the boil. Lower the heat, remove the lid and simmer for 20 minutes, stirring occasionally, until reduced.

3 Heat the oil in a frying pan. Add the mushrooms and remaining garlic. Season with salt and pepper to taste. Cook, stirring, for about 5 minutes, or until the mushrooms are tender. Set aside.

4 Preheat the oven to 220°C/425°F/Gas 7. Divide the pizza dough into four equal pieces. Roll out each piece on a lightly floured surface to a 25cm/10in round and place on four lightly oiled baking sheets.

5 Spoon the tomato sauce over each dough round and spread evenly over the surface to within 1cm/½in of the edge. Brush the edge with a little olive oil. Top the sauce with the mushrooms, fresh oregano and ricotta and Fontina cheeses.

6 Bake for about 15 minutes, until golden brown and crisp. Scatter the oregano leaves over the top.

Energy 862Kcal/3617kJ; Fat 40.7g; Saturated Fat 19.9g; Carbohydrate 94g; Fibre 5.7g

Rocket & Tomato Pizza

Peppery rocket and aromatic fresh basil add colour and flavour to this crisp pizza, a perfect addition to any picnic.

Serves 2
225g/8oz/2 cups strong white
   bread flour
5ml/1 tsp salt
2.5ml/½ tsp easy-blend
   (rapid-rise) dried yeast
30ml/2 tbsp olive oil
150ml/¼ pint/⅔ cup
   warm water

For the topping
10ml/2 tsp olive oil
1 garlic clove, crushed
150g/5oz canned chopped Italian
   plum tomatoes
2.5ml/½ tsp caster
   (superfine) sugar
30ml/2 tbsp torn fresh basil
2 tomatoes, seeded and chopped
150g/5oz mozzarella
   cheese, sliced
20g/¾oz rocket (arugula) leaves
salt and ground black pepper

1 To make the pizza base, place the dry ingredients in a bowl. Add the oil and the warm water. Mix to form a soft dough. Turn out the dough and knead until it is smooth and elastic. Place in an oiled bowl and cover. Leave in a warm place for 45 minutes, or until doubled in bulk.

2 Preheat the oven to 220°C/425°F/Gas 7. To make the topping, heat the oil in a frying pan and fry the garlic for 1 minute. Add the canned tomatoes and sugar and cook for 10 minutes, stirring occasionally.

3 Knead the risen dough lightly, then roll out to form a rough 30cm/12in round. Place on a lightly oiled baking sheet and push up the edges of the dough to form a shallow, even rim.

4 Season the tomato mixture and stir in the basil. Spoon on to the pizza base, then top with the fresh tomatoes. Arrange the mozzarella slices on top of the tomato mixture. Season with salt and pepper and drizzle with a little olive oil.

5 Bake for 10–12 minutes, until crisp and golden. Scatter the rocket leaves over the pizza just before serving.

Grilled Vegetable Pizza

Grilled vegetables are good at any time, but are particularly tasty when teamed with melted cheese.

Serves 4
1 courgette (zucchini), sliced
2 baby aubergines (eggplants) or
   1 small aubergine, sliced
30ml/2 tbsp olive oil
1 yellow (bell) pepper, seeded and
   thickly sliced
115g/4oz/1 cup cornmeal
50g/2oz/½ cup potato flour

50g/2oz/½ cup soya flour
5ml/1 tsp baking powder
2.5ml/½ tsp salt
50g/2oz/¼ cup butter or soft
   margarine
about 105ml/7 tbsp milk
4 plum tomatoes, peeled
   and chopped
30ml/2 tbsp chopped fresh basil
115g/4oz mozzarella
   cheese, sliced
salt and ground black pepper
fresh basil leaves, to garnish

1 Preheat the grill (broiler). Brush the sliced courgette and aubergine slices with a little oil and place on a grill rack with the pepper slices. Cook under the grill, until lightly browned, turning once.

2 Meanwhile, preheat the oven to 200°C/400°F/Gas 6. Place the cornmeal, potato flour, soya flour, baking powder and salt in a mixing bowl and stir to mix. Lightly rub in the butter or margarine until the mixture resembles coarse breadcrumbs. Stir in enough of the milk to make a soft but not sticky dough.

3 Place the dough on a sheet of non-stick baking parchment on a baking sheet and roll or press it out to form a 25cm/10in round, pushing up the edges to form a shallow, even rim.

4 Brush the pizza dough with any remaining oil, then spread the chopped tomatoes over the dough. Sprinkle with the chopped basil and season with salt and pepper. Arrange the grilled (broiled) vegetables over the tomatoes and top with the sliced mozzarella cheese.

5 Bake for 25–30 minutes, until crisp and golden brown. Garnish the pizza with fresh basil and serve immediately.

Energy 735Kcal/3087kJ; Fat 31.3g; Saturated Fat 12.7g; Carbohydrate 93g; Fibre 5.5g

Energy 400Kcal/1666kJ; Fat 23.9g; Saturated Fat 5.3g; Carbohydrate 34.6g; Fibre 4.4g

Radicchio & Olive Pizza

With its quick-to-make
scone dough base, this tasty
vegetable pizza is very easy
to prepare.

Serves 2
225g/8oz/2 cups self-raising
  (self-rising) flour
2.5ml/½ tsp salt
50g/2oz/¼ cup butter
about 120ml/4fl oz/½ cup milk

For the topping
400ml/14fl oz/1⅔ cups passata
  (bottled, strained tomatoes)

pinch of dried basil
2 garlic cloves, crushed
25ml/1½ tbsp olive oil, plus extra
  for dipping
2 leeks, sliced
100g/3½oz radicchio,
  roughly chopped
20g/¾oz Parmesan
  cheese, grated
115g/4oz mozzarella
  cheese, sliced
10–12 pitted black olives
salt and ground black pepper
fresh basil leaves, to garnish

1 Preheat the oven to 220°C/425°F/Gas 7 and grease a baking sheet. Mix the flour and salt in a bowl, rub in the butter and stir in enough milk to make a soft dough. Roll it out on a lightly floured surface to a 25–28cm/10–11in round. Place on the baking sheet.

2 Mix the passata, basil and half of the garlic in a small pan. Season with salt and pepper, then simmer over medium heat until the mixture is thick and has reduced by about half.

3 Heat the olive oil in a large frying pan and fry the leeks and remaining garlic for 4–5 minutes, until slightly softened. Add the radicchio and cook, stirring continuously for a few minutes, then cover and simmer gently for about 5–10 minutes. Stir in the Parmesan cheese and season to taste.

4 Cover the dough base with the passata mixture and then spoon the leek and radicchio mixture on top. Arrange the mozzarella slices on top and scatter with the black olives.

5 Dip a few basil leaves in olive oil, arrange on top and bake the pizza for 15–20 minutes, until the top is golden brown.

Onion Focaccia

This pizza-like flat bread is
characterized by its soft
dimpled surface, sometimes
dredged simply with coarse
salt, or with onions, herbs
or olives. It tastes delicious
served warm with soup.

Makes 2
675g/1½lb/6 cups strong plain
  bread flour
2.5ml/½ tsp salt

2.5ml/½ tsp caster
  (superfine) sugar
15ml/1 tbsp easy-blend
  (rapid-rise) dried yeast
60ml/4 tbsp extra virgin olive oil
450ml/¾ pint/scant 2 cups
  warm water

For the topping
2 red onions, thinly sliced
45ml/3 tbsp extra virgin olive oil
15ml/1 tbsp coarse salt

1 Sift the flour, salt and sugar into a large bowl. Stir in the yeast, oil and water and mix to a dough using a round-bladed knife. (Add a little extra water if the dough is dry.)

2 Turn out on to a lightly floured surface and knead for about 10 minutes, until smooth and elastic. Put the dough in a clean, lightly oiled bowl and cover with clear film (plastic wrap). Leave to rise in a warm place, until doubled in bulk.

3 Place two 25cm/10in plain metal flan rings on baking sheets. Oil the insides of the rings and the baking sheets.

4 Preheat the oven to 200°C/400°F/Gas 6. Halve the dough and roll each piece to a 25cm/10in round. Press into the flan rings, cover with a dampened dish cloth and leave for 30 minutes to rise.

5 Make deep holes, about 2.5cm/1in apart, in the dough. Cover and leave for a further 20 minutes.

6 To finish, scatter with the onions and drizzle over the oil. Sprinkle with the salt, then a little cold water, to stop a crust from forming. Bake the focaccia for about 25 minutes, lightly sprinkling with water again during cooking. Cool on a wire rack before serving.

Energy 970Kcal/4066kJ; Fat 52.4g; Saturated Fat 26g; Carbohydrate 99.4g; Fibre 8.5g

Energy 1508Kcal/6362kJ; Fat 42.9g; Saturated Fat 6.2g; Carbohydrate 264.6g; Fibre 10.9g

Mediterranean Pizza

The combination of favourite Mediterranean ingredients makes a delicious modern pizza topping. Serve with a mixed green salad for an easy lunch dish.

Serves 4
12 sun-dried tomatoes, dry or in oil, drained
1 quantity Basic Pizza Dough (see page 64)
flour, for dusting
350g/12oz/1¾ cups goat's cheese, sliced as thinly as possible
30ml/2 tbsp capers in brine or salt, rinsed
10 fresh basil leaves
60ml/4 tbsp olive oil
salt and ground black pepper

1 Preheat the oven to 240°C/475°F/Gas 9. To prepare the topping, if using dry sun-dried tomatoes, place in a small bowl, cover with hot water and leave to soak for 15 minutes. Drain and cut into thin slices. If using sun-dried tomatoes in oil, drain and slice thinly.

2 Roll out the pizza dough to a 30cm/12in round on a floured surface. Place on a large baking sheet.

3 Arrange the cheese on the pizza base, to within 1cm/½in of the edge. Dot the pizza with the tomato pieces.

4 Sprinkle with the capers and basil leaves. Allow to rise for 10 minutes before baking.

5 Sprinkle the pizza with salt, pepper and olive oil. Place the pizza in the oven. Bake for 20–30 minutes, or until golden.

> **Cook's Tips**
> • The soaking water from the sun-dried tomatoes can be saved for adding to a pasta sauce or soup.
> • For a more moist pizza, spread a thin layer of home-made tomato sauce on the base before add the topping ingredients.

Energy 489Kcal/2046kJ; Fat 26.9g; Saturated Fat 11.6g; Carbohydrate 46g; Fibre 2.3g

Vegetable Wholemeal Pizza

For a satisfying meal, serve this pizza with a mixed bean salad and crusty bread.

Serves 2
10ml/2 tsp olive oil
30ml/2 tbsp tomato purée (paste)
10ml/2 tsp dried basil
1 onion, sliced
1 garlic clove, finely chopped
2 small courgettes (zucchini), sliced
115g/4oz mushrooms, sliced
115g/4oz/⅔ cup canned or frozen sweetcorn
4 plum tomatoes, sliced
50g/2oz/½ cup grated Red Leicester cheese
50g/2oz mozzarella cheese, grated
salt and ground black pepper
basil sprigs, to garnish

For the pizza base
225g/8oz/2 cups plain (all-purpose) wholemeal (whole-wheat) flour
pinch of salt
10ml/2 tsp baking powder
50g/2oz/¼ cup margarine
about 150ml/¼ pint/⅔ cup milk

1 Preheat the oven to 220°C/425°F/Gas 7. Grease a baking sheet with a little oil. To make the pizza base, put the flour, salt and baking powder in a bowl and rub the margarine lightly into the flour until it resembles breadcrumbs. Add enough milk to form a soft dough and knead. Roll out to a 25cm/10in round.

2 Place the dough on the prepared baking sheet, then push up the edges to make a thin rim. Spread the tomato purée over the base and sprinkle the basil on top.

3 Heat the oil in a frying pan, add the onion, garlic, courgettes and mushrooms, and cook gently for 10 minutes, stirring occasionally. Spread the mixture over the pizza base, sprinkle the corn on top and season with salt and pepper. Arrange the tomato slices on top. Mix together the cheeses and sprinkle over the pizza. Bake for 25–30 minutes, until cooked.

Pizza with Onions & Olives

The sweetness of slow-cooked onions contrasts nicely with the tangy olives.

Serves 4
90ml/6 tbsp olive oil
4 onions, finely sliced
salt and ground black pepper
1 quantity Basic Pizza Dough (see page 64), rolled out to a 30cm/12in round
350g/12oz/1¾ cups diced mozzarella cheese
32 black olives, pitted and halved
45ml/3 tbsp chopped fresh parsley

1 Preheat the oven to 240°C/475°F/Gas 9. Heat half the olive oil in a large frying pan. Add the sliced onions and cook over low heat for 12–15 minutes, until soft and just beginning to turn brown. Season with salt and pepper and remove from the heat.

2 Spread the onions over the prepared pizza dough to within 1cm/½in of the edge. Sprinkle with the mozzarella. Dot with the olives. Sprinkle with parsley and the remaining olive oil and bake for 15–20 minutes, or until the crust is golden brown and the cheese is bubbling.

Top Energy 913Kcal/3833kJ; Fat 42.6g; Saturated Fat 11g; Carbohydrate 102g; Fibre 15.4g
Above Energy 551Kcal/2300kJ; Fat 30.8g; Saturated Fat 8g; Carbohydrate 57g; Fibre 4.8g

Classic Marinara Pizza

The combination of simple ingredients gives this pizza its truly Italian flavour.

Serves 2
60ml/4 tbsp extra virgin olive oil or sunflower oil
675g/1½lb plum tomatoes, peeled, seeded and chopped
4 garlic cloves, cut into slivers

15ml/1 tbsp chopped oregano
salt and ground black pepper

For the pizza base
225g/8oz/2 cups plain (all-purpose) flour
pinch of salt
10ml/2 tsp baking powder
50g/2oz/¼ cup margarine
about 150ml/¼ pint/⅔ cup milk

1 Preheat the oven to 220°C/425°F/Gas 7. Use non-stick baking parchment to line a baking sheet. To make the base, sieve (sift) the flour, salt and baking powder in a bowl and rub the margarine lightly into the flour until it resembles breadcrumbs.

2 Pour in enough milk to form a soft dough and knead. Roll the dough out to a circle about 25cm/10in in diameter. Place the dough on the prepared baking sheet, then push up the dough edges to make a thin rim.

3 Heat 30ml/2 tbsp of the oil in a pan. Add the tomatoes and cook, stirring for about 5 minutes, until soft. Place the tomatoes in a sieve (strainer) over a bowl and leave to drain for 5 minutes. Discard the juice in the bowl, then purée the flesh in the sieve.

4 Brush the pizza base with half the remaining oil. Spoon over the tomatoes and sprinkle with garlic and oregano. Drizzle over the remaining oil and season. Bake for 15–20 minutes in

Pizza with Four Cheeses

Any combination of cheeses can be used, but they must be different in character.

Serves 4
1 quantity Basic Pizza Dough (see page 64), rolled out
75g/3oz/½ cup Gorgonzola or other blue cheese, thinly sliced
75g/3oz/½ cup diced mozzarella cheese

75g/3oz/½ cup goat's cheese, thinly sliced
7g/3oz/½ cup grated mature (sharp) Cheddar cheese
4 fresh sage leaves, torn into pieces, or 45ml/3tbsp chopped fresh parsley
salt and ground black pepper
45ml/3 tbsp olive oil

1 Preheat the oven to 240°C/475°F/Gas 9. Arrange the Gorgonzola on one quarter of the pizza and the mozzarella on another, leaving the edge free.

2 Arrange the goat's and Cheddar cheeses on the remaining two quarters.

3 Sprinkle with the herbs, salt and pepper, and olive oil. Bake for about 15–20 minutes, or until the crust is golden brown and the cheeses are bubbling.

Pizza with Sausage

In unfussy Italian style, sausagemeat, tomatoes and mozzarella are simply flavoured with oregano to make a mouthwatering pizza.

Serves 4
450g/1lb drained, peeled plum tomatoes, fresh or canned
225g/8oz/1½ cups Italian sausages

1 quantity Basic Pizza Dough (see page 64)
flour, for dusting
350g/12oz/1¾ cups diced mozzarella cheese
5ml/1 tsp oregano leaves, fresh or dried
45ml/3 tbsp olive oil
salt and ground black pepper

1 Preheat the oven to 240°C/475°F/Gas 9. Strain the tomatoes through the medium holes of a food mill or sieve (strainer) placed over a bowl, scraping in all the pulp.

2 Snip the end off the sausage skin and squeeze out the sausagemeat.

2 Roll out the dough on a lightly floured surface to a 30cm/12in round. Place on a baking sheet.

3 Spread some of the puréed tomatoes on the prepared pizza dough, leaving the rim uncovered. Sprinkle evenly with the mozzarella. Add the sausagemeat in small lumps.

4 Sprinkle with oregano, salt and pepper, and olive oil. Bake for about 15–20 minutes, or until the crust is golden brown and the cheese is bubbling.

> **Cook's Tip**
> For the best flavour, try to find salsiccia (fresh Italian-style sausage) from Italian delicatessens. Salsiccia puro suino is the best. If you have difficulty finding salsiccia, you can substitute good-quality sausages with a high meat content; ones flavoured with herbs or spices will add zing to the topping.

Top Energy 429Kcal/1798kJ; Fat 23g; Saturated Fat 2.3g; Carbohydrate 50.8g; Fibre 3.4g
Above Energy 546Kcal/2283kJ; Fat 32g; Saturated Fat 15g; Carbohydrate 43.7g; Fibre 1.6g

Energy 632Kcal/2641kJ; Fat 37.9g; Saturated Fat 14g; Carbohydrate 55.4g; Fibre 3.1g

Pumpkin & Pistachio Risotto

An elegant combination of creamy, golden rice and orange pumpkin, this stunning risotto is Italian cooking at its best.

Serves 4
1.2 litres/2 pints/5 cups vegetable
   stock or water
generous pinch of saffron threads
30ml/2 tbsp olive oil
1 onion, chopped
2 garlic cloves, crushed
900g/2lb pumpkin, peeled, seeded
   and cut into 2cm/¾in cubes

400g/14oz/2 cups risotto rice
200ml/7fl oz/scant 1 cup dry
   white wine
30ml/2 tbsp freshly grated
   Parmesan cheese
50g/2oz/½ cup pistachios,
   coarsely chopped
45ml/3 tbsp chopped fresh
   marjoram or oregano, plus
   leaves to garnish
salt, freshly grated nutmeg and
   ground black pepper

1 Bring the stock or water to the boil and reduce to a low simmer. Ladle a little of it into a small bowl. Add the saffron threads and leave to infuse.

2 Heat the oil in a large, heavy pan or deep frying pan. Add the onion and garlic and cook gently for about 5 minutes, until softened. Add the pumpkin cubes and rice and stir to coat everything in oil. Cook for a few more minutes, until the rice looks transparent.

3 Pour in the wine and allow it to bubble hard. When it has been absorbed, add a quarter of the hot stock or water and the saffron liquid. Stir until all the liquid has been absorbed. Gradually add the remaining stock or water, a little at a time, allowing the rice to absorb the liquid before adding more, and stirring constantly. After 20–30 minutes the rice should be golden yellow, creamy and al dente.

4 Stir in the Parmesan cheese, cover the pan and leave to stand for 5 minutes. To finish, stir in the pistachios and marjoram or oregano. Season to taste with a little salt, nutmeg and pepper, and scatter over a few marjoram or oregano leaves.

Energy 589Kcal/2458kJ; Fat 16g; Saturated Fat 3.5g; Carbohydrate 87.6g; Fibre 3.9g

Risotto with Parmesan

This traditional risotto is simply flavoured with grated Parmesan cheese and golden, fried chopped onion.

Serves 3–4
1 litre/1¾ pints/4 cups beef,
   chicken or vegetable stock
65g/2½oz/5 tbsp butter

1 small onion, finely chopped
275g/10oz/1½ cups risotto rice
120ml/4fl oz/½ cup dry
   white wine
75g/3oz/1 cup freshly grated
   Parmesan cheese, plus extra
   to garnish
salt and ground black pepper
basil leaves, to garnish

1 Heat the stock in a pan and leave to simmer until needed.

2 Melt two-thirds of the butter in a large heavy pan or deep frying pan. Stir in the chopped onion and cook gently until softened and golden.

3 Add the risotto rice and stir to coat the grains with butter. After 1–2 minutes, pour in the white wine. Increase the heat slightly and cook until the wine evaporates. Add one small ladleful of the hot stock. Cook until the stock has been absorbed, stirring constantly.

4 Gradually add the remaining stock, a little at a time, allowing the rice to absorb the liquid before adding more, and stirring constantly. After 20–30 minutes the rice should be creamy and al dente. Season to taste.

5 Remove the pan from the heat. Stir in the remaining butter and the Parmesan cheese. Taste again for seasoning. Allow the risotto to stand for 3–4 minutes before serving, garnished with basil leaves and shavings of Parmesan, if you like.

Cook's Tip
If you run out of stock when cooking the risotto, just continue using hot water. Do not worry if the rice is done before all the stock is used up: only add as much as you need.

Energy 479Kcal/1991kJ; Fat 19.9g; Saturated Fat 12.3g; Carbohydrate 56.3g; Fibre 0.2g

Risotto with Ricotta & Basil

This is a well-flavoured risotto, which benefits from the distinct pungency of basil, mellowed with smooth, mild ricotta.

Serves 3–4

1 litre/1¾ pints/4 cups chicken or vegetable stock
45ml/3 tbsp olive oil
1 onion, finely chopped
275g/10oz/1½ cups risotto rice
175g/6oz/¾ cup ricotta cheese
50g/2oz/generous 1 cup fresh basil leaves, finely chopped, plus extra to garnish
75g/3oz/1 cup freshly grated Parmesan cheese
salt and ground black pepper

1 Heat the stock in a pan and leave to simmer. Heat the oil in a large heavy pan and fry the onion over gentle heat until soft.

2 Stir in the rice. Cook for a few minutes, stirring, until the rice is coated with oil and is slightly translucent.

3 Pour in about a quarter of the stock. Cook, stirring, until all the stock has been absorbed. Gradually add the remaining stock, a ladleful at a time, allowing the rice to absorb the liquid before adding more, and stirring constantly. After 20–30 minutes the rice should be creamy and al dente. Season to taste with salt and pepper.

4 Spoon the ricotta into a bowl and break it up a little with a fork. Stir into the risotto along with the basil and Parmesan. Taste and adjust the seasoning, then cover and allow to stand for 2–3 minutes before serving, garnished with basil leaves.

> **Cook's Tip**
> The short grain rice that grows in the Po Valley in Piedmont is ideal for the slow cooking method used in risottos. The grains are able to absorb all the cooking liquid, acquiring a creamy smoothness while at the same time retaining their shape. The three types of risotto rice to look out for in Italian delicatessens are Carnaroli, Arborio and Vialone Nano.

Energy 494Kcal/2055kJ; Fat 21.3g; Saturated Fat 9g; Carbohydrate 57.8g; Fibre 0.8g

Rosemary Risotto with Borlotti Beans

This is a classic risotto with a subtle and complex taste, from the heady flavours of rosemary to the savoury beans and the fruity-sweet flavours of mascarpone and Parmesan.

Serves 3–4

400g/14oz can borlotti beans
30ml/2 tbsp olive oil
1 onion, chopped
2 garlic cloves, crushed
275g/10oz/1½ cups risotto rice
175ml/6fl oz/¾ cup dry white wine
900ml–1 litre/1½–1¾ pints/3¾–4 cups simmering vegetable or chicken stock
60ml/4 tbsp mascarpone cheese
65g/2½oz/scant 1 cup freshly grated Parmesan cheese, plus extra, to serve (optional)
5ml/1 tsp chopped fresh rosemary
salt and ground black pepper

1 Drain the beans, rinse under cold water and drain again. Purée about two-thirds of the beans fairly coarsely in a food processor or blender. Set the remaining beans aside.

2 Heat the olive oil in a large pan and gently fry the onion and garlic for 6–8 minutes, until very soft. Add the rice and cook over a medium heat for a few minutes, stirring constantly, until the grains are thoroughly coated in oil and are slightly translucent.

3 Pour in the wine. Cook over medium heat for 2–3 minutes, stirring all the time, until the wine has been absorbed. Add the stock gradually, a ladleful at a time, allowing the rice to absorb the liquid before adding more, and continuing to stir.

4 When the rice is three-quarters cooked, stir in the bean purée. Continue to cook the risotto, adding the remaining stock, until it is creamy and the rice is al dente. Add the reserved beans, with the mascarpone, Parmesan and rosemary, then season to taste. Stir, then cover and leave to stand for about 5 minutes so that the rice completes cooking and absorbs all the flavours. Serve with extra Parmesan, if you like.

Energy 362Kcal/1517kJ; Fat 20g; Saturated Fat 8g; Carbohydrate 38g; Fibre 65g

Porcini & Parmesan Risotto

This variation on the classic Risotto alla Milanese includes saffron, porcini mushrooms and Parmesan.

Serves 4

15g/½oz/2 tbsp dried
  porcini mushrooms
150ml/¼ pint/⅔ cup
  warm water
1 litre/1¾ pints/4 cups
  vegetable stock
generous pinch of saffron threads

30ml/2 tbsp olive oil
1 onion, finely chopped
1 garlic clove, crushed
350g/12oz/1¾ cups risotto rice
150ml/¼ pint/⅔ cup dry
  white wine
25g/1oz/2 tbsp butter
50g/2oz/⅔ cup freshly grated
  Parmesan cheese
salt and ground black pepper
pink and yellow oyster
  mushrooms, to serve (optional)

1 Put the dried porcini in a bowl and pour over the warm water. Leave the mushrooms to soak for 20 minutes, then lift out with a slotted spoon. Filter the soaking water through a layer of kitchen paper in a sieve (strainer), then place it in a pan with the stock. Bring the liquid to a gentle simmer.

2 Spoon about 45ml/3 tbsp of the hot stock into a cup and stir in the saffron strands. Set aside. Finely chop the porcini. Heat the oil in a separate pan and lightly sauté the onion, garlic and mushrooms for 5 minutes. Gradually add the rice, stirring to coat the grains in oil. Cook for 2 minutes, stirring constantly. Season with salt and pepper.

3 Pour in the white wine. Cook, stirring, until it has been absorbed, then ladle in a quarter of the stock. Cook, stirring, until the stock has been absorbed. Gradually add the remaining stock, a little at a time, allowing the rice to absorb the liquid before adding more, and stirring constantly.

4 After about 20 minutes, when all the stock has been absorbed and the rice is cooked but still al dente, stir in the butter, saffron water (with the strands) and half the Parmesan. Serve, sprinkled with the remaining Parmesan. Garnish with pink and yellow oyster mushrooms, if you like.

Risotto with Four Vegetables

This is one of the prettiest risottos; fresh green vegetables highlight the sweet yellow squash.

Serves 3–4

115g/4oz/1 cup shelled
  fresh peas
115g/4oz/1 cup green beans, cut
  into short lengths
1 litre/1¾ pints/4 cups
  chicken stock

30ml/2 tbsp olive oil
75g/3oz/6 tbsp butter
1 acorn squash, skin and seeds
  removed, cut into matchsticks
1 onion, finely chopped
275g/10oz/1½ cups risotto rice
120ml/4fl oz/½ cup Italian dry
  white vermouth
75g/3oz/1 cup freshly grated
  Parmesan cheese
salt and ground black pepper

1 Bring a pan of lightly salted water to the boil, add the peas and beans and cook for 2–3 minutes, until the vegetables are just tender. Drain, refresh under cold running water, drain again and set aside. Bring the stock to a simmer in a pan.

2 Heat the oil with 25g/1oz/2 tbsp of the butter in a medium pan until foaming. Add the squash and cook gently for 2–3 minutes or until just softened. Remove with a slotted spoon and set aside. Add the onion to the pan and cook gently for about 3 minutes, stirring frequently, until softened.

3 Stir in the rice until the grains start to swell and burst, then add the vermouth. Stir until the vermouth stops sizzling and most of it has been absorbed by the rice, then add a few ladlefuls of the stock, with salt and pepper to taste. Stir over low heat, until the stock has been absorbed.

4 Gradually add the remaining stock, a few ladlefuls at a time, allowing the rice to absorb the liquid before adding more, and stirring all the time. After about 20 minutes, when all the stock has been absorbed and the rice is cooked and creamy but still al dente, gently stir in the vegetables, the remaining butter and about half the grated Parmesan. Heat through, then taste for seasoning and serve with the remaining grated Parmesan served separately.

Energy 497Kcal/2069kJ; Fat 15.2g; Saturated Fat 6.6g; Carbohydrate 71.3g; Fibre 0.2g

Energy 624Kcal/2611kJ; Fat 31.2g; Saturated Fat 14.6g; Carbohydrate 63.9g; Fibre 3.5g

Green Risotto

You could use spinach-flavoured risotto rice to give this stunning dish even greater dramatic impact. However, white risotto rice makes a pretty contrast to the spinach.

Serves 3–4

1 litre/1¾ pints/4 cups chicken stock
30ml/2 tbsp olive oil
1 onion, finely chopped
275g/10oz/1½ cups risotto rice
75ml/5 tbsp white wine
about 400g/14oz tender baby spinach leaves
15ml/1 tbsp chopped fresh basil
5ml/1 tsp chopped fresh mint
60ml/4 tbsp freshly grated Parmesan cheese
salt and ground black pepper
knob of butter or more grated Parmesan cheese, to serve

1 Heat the stock in a pan and leave to simmer until needed.

2 Heat the oil in a heavy pan and fry the onion for 3–4 minutes until soft. Add the rice and stir to coat each grain. Pour in the white wine. Cook, stirring, until it has been absorbed.

3 Add a few ladlefuls of the stock and cook, stirring, until the stock has been absorbed. Gradually add the remaining stock, a little at a time, allowing the rice to absorb the liquid before adding more, and stirring constantly.

4 Stir in the spinach leaves and herbs with the last of the liquid, and add a little salt and pepper. Continue cooking until the rice is cooked but still al dente and the spinach leaves have wilted. Stir in the Parmesan cheese, with a knob of butter, if you like, or serve with extra Parmesan.

> **Cook's Tip**
> *The secret to risotto is to add the hot liquid gradually, about a ladleful at a time, and to stir constantly until the liquid has been absorbed before adding more. It is easy to overcook Arborio rice and it is often recommended to turn off the heat when the risotto is almost cooked and 'resting' for a few minutes.*

Oven-baked Porcini Risotto

This risotto is easy to make because you don't have to stand over it, stirring constantly as it cooks, as you do with a traditional risotto.

Serves 4

25g/1oz/½ cup dried porcini mushrooms
30ml/2 tbsp garlic-infused olive oil
1 onion, finely chopped
225g/8oz/generous 1 cup risotto rice
salt and ground black pepper

1 Put the porcini mushrooms in a heatproof bowl and pour over 750ml/1½ pints/3 cups boiling water. Leave them to soak for 30 minutes. Drain the mushrooms through a sieve (strainer) lined with kitchen paper, reserving the soaking liquor. Rinse the mushrooms thoroughly under cold running water to remove any grit, and dry on kitchen paper.

2 Preheat the oven to 180°C/350°F/Gas 4. Heat the olive oil in a large roasting pan on the hob on medium heat and add the chopped onion. Cook for 2–3 minutes, or until softened but not coloured.

3 Add the risotto rice and stir for 1–2 minutes, then add the reserved mushrooms and stir well. Pour in the mushroom liquor and mix thoroughly. Season with salt and pepper to taste, and cover with foil.

4 Bake in the oven for 30 minutes, stirring occasionally, until all the stock has been absorbed and the rice is tender. Divide between warm serving bowls and serve immediately.

> **Cook's Tip**
> *In Italy, porcini mushrooms are used all year round, not as a substitute for fresh porcini, but as a valued ingredient in its own right. Don't buy cheap porcini, but look for packets containing large pale-coloured pieces. Although they will seem expensive, a little goes a long way.*

Energy 363Kcal/1515kJ; Fat 6.7g; Saturated Fat 3.3g; Carbohydrate 57.8g; Fibre 2.5g

Energy 288Kcal/1218kJ; Fat 8g; Saturated Fat 1g; Carbohydrate 52g; Fibre 1.6g

Brown Rice Risotto with Mushrooms

A classic risotto of mixed mushrooms, herbs and fresh Parmesan cheese, but made using brown long-grain rice. Serve with a mixed leaf salad tossed in a balsamic dressing for a stylish lunch.

Serves 4
15g/½oz/2 tbsp dried
    porcini mushrooms
150ml/¼ pint/⅔ cup
    warm water
15ml/1 tbsp olive oil
4 shallots, finely chopped
2 garlic cloves, crushed
250g/9oz/1⅓ cups brown
    long-grain rice
900ml/1½ pints/3¾ cups well-
    flavoured vegetable stock
450g/1lb/6 cups mixed
    mushrooms, such as closed cup,
    chestnut and field mushrooms,
    sliced if large
30–45ml/2–3 tbsp chopped fresh
    flat leaf parsley
50g/2oz/⅔ cup freshly grated
    Parmesan cheese
salt and ground black pepper

1 Put the dried porcini in a bowl and pour over the warm water. Leave the mushrooms to soak for 20 minutes, then lift out with a slotted spoon. Filter the soaking water through a layer of kitchen paper in a sieve (strainer) and reserve. Roughly chop the porcini.

2 Heat the oil in a large pan, add the shallots and garlic and cook gently for 5 minutes, stirring. Add the brown rice to the shallot mixture and stir to coat the grains in oil.

3 Stir the vegetable stock and the porcini soaking liquid into the rice mixture in the pan. Bring to the boil, lower the heat and simmer, uncovered, for about 20 minutes, or until most of the liquid has been absorbed, stirring frequently.

4 Add all the mushrooms, stir well and cook the risotto for a further 10–15 minutes, until the liquid has been absorbed.

5 Season with salt and pepper to taste, stir in the chopped parsley and grated Parmesan and serve immediately.

Two Cheese Risotto

This deliciously rich and creamy risotto is just the thing to serve on cold winter evenings when everyone needs warming up.

Serves 3–4
1 litre/3¾ pints/4 cups vegetable
    or chicken stock
7.5ml/1½ tsp olive oil
50g/2oz/¼ cup butter
1 onion, finely chopped
1 garlic clove, crushed
275g/10oz/1½ cups risotto rice,
    preferably Vialone Nano
175ml/6fl oz/¾ cup dry
    white wine
75g/3oz/¾ cup Fontina
    cheese, cubed
50g/2oz/⅔ cup freshly grated
    Parmesan cheese, plus extra,
    to serve
salt and ground black pepper

1 Heat the stock in a pan and leave to simmer until needed.

2 Heat the olive oil with half the butter in a pan and gently fry the onion and garlic for 5–6 minutes, until soft. Add the rice and cook, stirring all the time, until the grains are coated in fat and have become slightly translucent around the edges.

3 Pour in the white wine. Cook, stirring, until it has been absorbed, then add a ladleful of hot stock. Cook, stirring, until the stock has been absorbed. Gradually add the remaining stock, a little at a time, allowing the rice to absorb the liquid before adding more, and stirring constantly.

4 When the rice is half cooked, stir in the Fontina cheese, and continue cooking and adding stock gradually. Keep stirring.

5 When the risotto is creamy and the grains are tender but still al dente, stir in the remaining butter and the Parmesan. Season with salt and pepper, then remove the pan from the heat. Cover and leave to stand for 3–4 minutes before serving.

> **Variation**
> Stir in a handful of chopped fresh herbs with the Parmesan.

Energy 547Kcal/2273kJ; Fat 25.1g; Saturated Fat 13.8g; Carbohydrate 56.4g; Fibre 0.2g

Energy 338Kcal/1412kJ; Fat 7.8g; Saturated Fat 3.1g; Carbohydrate 54.3g; Fibre 2g

Champagne Risotto

This may seem rather extravagant, but it makes a really beautifully flavoured risotto, perfect for that special anniversary dinner.

Serves 3–4
750ml/1¼ pints/3 cups light vegetable or chicken stock
25g/1oz/2 tbsp butter
2 shallots, finely chopped
275g/10oz/1½ cups risotto rice, preferably Carnaroli
½ bottle or 300ml/½ pint/1¼ cups champagne
150ml/¼ pint/⅔ cup double (heavy) cream
40g/1½oz/½ cup freshly grated Parmesan cheese
10ml/2 tsp very finely chopped fresh chervil
salt and ground black pepper
black truffle shavings, to garnish (optional)

1 Heat the stock in a pan and leave to simmer until needed.

2 Melt the butter in a pan and fry the shallots for 2–3 minutes until softened. Add the rice and cook, stirring all the time, until the grains are evenly coated in butter and are beginning to look translucent around the edges.

3 Pour in about two-thirds of the champagne and cook over a high heat so that the liquid bubbles fiercely. Cook, stirring constantly, until all the liquid has been absorbed, then begin to add the hot stock.

4 Add the stock, a ladleful at a time, making sure that each addition has been completely absorbed before adding the next. The risotto should gradually become creamy and velvety and all the stock should be absorbed.

5 When the rice is tender but still *al dente*, stir in the remaining champagne and the double cream and grated Parmesan. Taste for seasoning.

6 Remove from the heat, cover and leave to stand for a few minutes. Stir in the chervil and serve topped with a few truffle shavings, if you like.

Energy 468Kcal/1941kJ; Fat 23.1g; Saturated Fat 14.3g; Carbohydrate 48.3g; Fibre 0.1g

Fried Rice Balls Stuffed with Mozzarella

These deep-fried balls of risotto are stuffed with mozzarella cheese. They are very popular snacks in Italy, which is hardly surprising as they are quite delicious.

Serves 4
1 quantity Risotto with Parmesan (see page 74)
3 eggs
115g/4oz/⅔ cup diced mozzarella cheese
oil, for deep-frying
breadcrumbs and flour, to coat
dressed frisée lettuce and cherry tomatoes, to serve

1 Put the risotto in a bowl and allow it to cool completely. Beat two of the eggs together, then stir them into the cold risotto.

2 Use your hands to form the rice mixture into balls the size of a large egg. If the mixture is too moist to hold its shape well, stir in a few tablespoons of breadcrumbs. Poke a hole into the centre of each ball with your finger, then fill it with a few small cubes of mozzarella, and close the hole over again with the rice mixture.

3 Heat the oil for deep-frying until a small piece of bread sizzles as soon as it is dropped in.

4 Spread some flour on a plate. Beat the remaining egg in a shallow bowl. Sprinkle another plate with breadcrumbs. Roll the balls in the flour, then in the egg, and finally in the breadcrumbs.

5 Fry them a few at a time in the hot oil, until golden and crisp. Drain on kitchen paper while the remaining balls are being fried. Serve hot, with a salad of frisée lettuce and tomatoes.

Cook's Tip
This is the perfect way to use leftover risotto.

Energy 505Kcal/2111kJ; Fat 30.9g; Saturated Fat 8.5g; Carbohydrate 44.8g; Fibre 0.7g

Pesto Risotto

If you buy the pesto – and there are some excellent varieties available nowadays from Italian delicatessens – this is just about as easy as a risotto gets.

Serves 3–4
1 litre/1¾ pints/4 cups
  vegetable stock
30ml/2 tbsp olive oil
2 shallots, finely chopped
1 garlic clove, crushed
275g/10oz/1½ cups risotto rice
175ml/6fl oz/¾ cup dry white
  wine
45ml/3 tbsp pesto sauce
25g/1oz/⅓ cup freshly grated
  Parmesan cheese, plus extra,
  to serve (optional)
salt and ground black pepper

1 Heat the stock in a pan and leave to simmer until needed.

2 Heat the olive oil in a pan and fry the shallots and garlic for 4–5 minutes, until the shallots are soft but not browned.

3 Add the rice and cook over medium heat, stirring all the time, until the grains of rice are coated in oil and the outer part of the grain is translucent and the inner part opaque.

4 Pour in the wine. Cook, stirring, until all of it has been absorbed, then add a ladleful of the hot stock. Cook, stirring, until the stock has been absorbed. Gradually add the remaining stock, a little at a time, allowing the rice to absorb the liquid before adding more, and stirring constantly.

5 After about 20 minutes, when all the stock has been absorbed and the rice is creamy and tender but al dente, stir in the pesto and Parmesan. Taste and add salt and pepper to taste, then cover and leave to stand for 3–4 minutes. Spoon into a bowl and serve, with extra Parmesan, if you like.

Variation
Green basil pesto sauce is used for this recipe, but red pesto, made with red peppers, can also be used.

Pumpkin & Apple Risotto

Pumpkin and other winter squash appear in many classic Italian recipes. If pumpkins are out of season, butternut or onion squash work well as a substitute.

Serves 3–4
225g/8oz butternut squash
  or pumpkin flesh, peeled
  and seeded
1 cooking apple
25g/1oz/2 tbsp butter
900ml–1 litre/1½–1¾
  pints/3¾–4 cups
  vegetable stock
25ml/1½ tbsp olive oil
1 onion, finely chopped
1 garlic clove, crushed
275g/10oz/1½ cups risotto rice,
  such as Vialone Nano
175ml/6fl oz/¾ cup fruity
  white wine
75g/3oz/1 cup freshly grated
  Parmesan cheese
salt and ground black pepper

1 Cut the squash into small pieces. Peel, core and roughly chop the apple. Place in a pan and pour in 120ml/4fl oz/½ cup water. Bring to the boil, then simmer for 15–20 minutes, until the squash is very tender. Drain, return the squash mixture to the pan and add half the butter. Mash the mixture roughly with a fork to break up any large pieces, but leave the mixture chunky.

2 Heat the stock in a pan and leave to simmer until needed.

3 Heat the oil and remaining butter in a pan and fry the onion and garlic until the onion is soft. Add the rice and cook, stirring constantly, over medium heat for 2 minutes, until the rice is coated in oil and the grains are slightly translucent.

4 Add the wine and stir into the rice. When all the liquid has been absorbed, begin to add the stock a ladleful at a time, making sure each addition has been absorbed before adding the next. This should take about 20 minutes.

5 When roughly two ladlefuls of stock are left, add the squash and apple mixture together with another addition of stock. Continue to cook, stirring well and adding the rest of the stock, until the risotto is very creamy. Stir in the Parmesan, season to taste and serve immediately.

Energy 421Kcal/1751kJ; Fat 14.1g; Saturated Fat 3.2g; Carbohydrate 56.5g; Fibre 0.3g

Energy 439Kcal/1831kJ; Fat 13.3g; Saturated Fat 7.4g; Carbohydrate 59.1g; Fibre 1.1g

Roasted Pepper Risotto

The smoky flavour of the chargrilled red peppers gives this risotto a divinely earthy taste.

Serves 3–4
1 red (bell) pepper
1 yellow (bell) pepper
1 litre/1¾ pints/4 cups
    vegetable stock
15ml/1 tbsp olive oil
25g/1oz/2 tbsp butter
1 onion, chopped
2 garlic cloves, crushed
275g/10oz/1½ cups risotto rice
50g/2oz/²⁄₃ cup freshly grated
    Parmesan cheese
salt and ground black pepper
freshly grated Parmesan cheese,
    to serve (optional)

1 Preheat the grill (broiler) to high. Cut the peppers in half, remove the seeds and cores and arrange, cut-side down, on a baking sheet. Place under the grill for 5–6 minutes, until the skin is charred. Put the peppers in a plastic bag, tie the ends and leave for 4–5 minutes.

2 Peel the peppers when they are cool enough to handle and the steam has loosened the skin. Cut into thin strips. Bring the stock to the boil in a pan and leave to simmer until required.

3 Heat the oil and butter in a pan and fry the onion and garlic for 4–5 minutes over low heat, until the onion begins to soften. Add the peppers and cook the mixture for a further 3–4 minutes, stirring occasionally.

4 Stir in the rice. Cook over medium heat for 3–4 minutes, stirring all the time, until the rice is evenly coated in oil and the outer part of each grain has become translucent.

5 Add a ladleful of stock. Cook, stirring, until all the liquid has been absorbed. Continue to add the stock, a ladleful at a time, making sure that each quantity has been absorbed before adding the next.

6 When the rice is tender but is still al dente, stir in the Parmesan and season to taste. Cover and leave to stand for 3–4 minutes, then serve, with extra Parmesan, if using.

Jerusalem Artichoke Risotto

This is a simple and warming risotto, which benefits from the delicious and distinctive flavour of Jerusalem artichokes.

Serves 3–4
400g/14oz Jerusalem artichokes
40g/1½oz/3 tbsp butter
1 litre/1¾ pints/4 cups
    vegetable stock
15ml/1 tbsp olive oil
1 onion, finely chopped
1 garlic clove, crushed
275g/10oz/1½ cups risotto rice
120ml/4fl oz/½ cup fruity
    white wine
10ml/2 tsp fresh thyme,
    finely chopped
40g/1½oz/½ cup freshly grated
    Parmesan cheese, plus extra,
    to serve
salt and ground black pepper
fresh thyme sprigs, to garnish

1 Peel the artichokes, cut them into pieces and immediately add them to a pan of lightly salted water. Simmer them until tender, then drain and mash with 15g/½oz/1 tbsp of the butter. Add a little more salt, if needed.

2 Boil the stock in a pan and leave to simmer until required.

3 Heat the oil and the remaining butter in a pan and fry the onion and garlic for 5–6 minutes, until soft. Add the rice and cook over a medium heat for about 2 minutes, until the grains are translucent around the edges.

4 Pour in the wine, stir until it has been absorbed, then start adding the simmering stock, a ladleful at a time, making sure each quantity has been absorbed before adding the next.

5 When you have just one ladleful of stock to add, stir in the mashed artichokes and the chopped thyme. Season with salt and pepper. Continue cooking until the risotto is creamy and the artichokes are hot.

6 Stir in the Parmesan cheese. Remove from the heat, cover the pan and leave the risotto to stand for a few minutes. Spoon into a warmed serving dish, garnish with fresh thyme and serve with Parmesan.

Energy 362Kcal/1509kJ; Fat 7.6g; Saturated Fat 3.1g; Carbohydrate 61.7g; Fibre 1.6g

Energy 418Kcal/1741kJ; Fat 14.8g; Saturated Fat 7.7g; Carbohydrate 56g; Fibre 1.1g

Risotto with Asparagus

Fresh farm asparagus only has a short season, so make the most of it with this elegant risotto.

Serves 3–4
225g/8oz fresh asparagus
750ml/1¼ pints/3 cups vegetable
   or chicken stock

65g/2½oz/5 tbsp butter
1 small onion, finely chopped
275g/10oz/1½ cups risotto rice,
   such as Arborio or Carnaroli
75g/3oz/1 cup freshly grated
   Parmesan cheese
salt and ground black pepper

1 Bring a pan of water to the boil. Cut off any woody pieces on the ends of the asparagus stalks, peel the lower portions, then cook in the water for 5 minutes. Drain the asparagus, reserving the cooking water, refresh under cold water and drain again. Cut the asparagus diagonally into 4cm/1¼in pieces. Keep the tip and next-highest sections separate from the stalks.

2 Place the stock in a pan and add 450ml/¾ pint/scant 2 cups of the asparagus cooking water. Heat to simmering point and keep it hot.

3 Melt two-thirds of the butter in a large, heavy pan or deep frying pan. Add the onion and fry until it is soft and golden. Stir in all the asparagus except the top two sections. Cook for 2–3 minutes. Add the rice and cook for 1–2 minutes, mixing well to coat it with butter.

4 Stir in a ladleful of the hot liquid. Using a wooden spoon, stir until the stock has been absorbed. Gradually add the remaining stock, a little at a time, allowing the rice to absorb the liquid before adding more, and stirring all the time.

5 After 10 minutes, add the remaining asparagus sections. Continue to cook as before, for about 15 minutes, until the rice is al dente and the risotto is creamy.

6 Off the heat, stir in the remaining butter and the Parmesan. Grind in a little black pepper, and taste again for salt. Serve.

Energy 467Kcal/1940kJ; Fat 20.2g; Saturated Fat 12.4g; Carbohydrate 56.1g; Fibre 1g

Risotto with Four Cheeses

This is a very rich, heady dish, made with four flavourful Italian cheeses. Serve it for a special dinner-party first course, with a light, dry sparkling white wine.

Serves 4
40g/1½oz/3 tbsp butter
1 small onion, finely chopped
1.2 litres/2 pints/5 cups
   chicken stock
350g/12oz/1¾ cups risotto rice

200ml/7fl oz/scant 1cup dry
   white wine
50g/2oz/½ cup grated
   Gruyère cheese
50g/2oz/½ cup diced
   taleggio cheese
50g/2oz/½ cup diced
   Gorgonzola cheese
50g/2oz/⅔ cup freshly grated
   Parmesan cheese
salt and ground black pepper
chopped fresh flat leaf parsley,
   to garnish

1 Melt the butter in a large, heavy pan or deep frying pan and fry the onion over gentle heat for about 4–5 minutes, stirring frequently, until softened and lightly browned.

2 Pour the stock into another pan and heat it to simmering point. Keep simmering until required.

3 Add the rice to the onion mixture, and stir until the grains of rice are coated in oil and the outer part of the grain is translucent and the inner part opaque. Add the wine. Stir until it stops sizzling and most of it has been absorbed by the rice, then pour in a little of the hot stock. Add salt and pepper to taste. Stir over low heat, until the stock has been absorbed.

4 Gradually add the remaining stock, a ladleful at a time, allowing the rice to absorb the liquid before adding more, and stirring constantly. After 20–25 minutes the rice should be al dente and the risotto creamy.

5 Turn off the heat under the pan, then add the Gruyère, taleggio, Gorgonzola and 30ml/2 tbsp of the Parmesan. Stir gently until the cheeses have melted, then taste for seasoning. Garnish with parsley and serve with the remaining Parmesan.

Energy 630Kcal/2624kJ; Fat 24.6g; Saturated Fat 15.6g; Carbohydrate 71.4g; Fibre 0.2g

Leek, Mushroom & Lemon Risotto

Leeks and lemon go together beautifully in this light risotto, while brown cap mushrooms add texture and extra flavour.

Serves 4
225g/8oz trimmed leeks
1.2 litres/2 pints/5 cups
  vegetable stock
30ml/2 tbsp olive oil
3 garlic cloves, crushed

225g/8oz/2–3 cups brown cap
  mushrooms, chopped roughly
75g/3oz/6 tbsp butter
1 large onion, roughly chopped
350g/12oz/1¾ cups risotto rice
  grated rind of 1 lemon
45ml/3 tbsp lemon juice
50g/2oz/²⁄₃ cup freshly grated
  Parmesan cheese
60ml/4 tbsp mixed chopped fresh
  chives and flat leaf parsley
salt and ground black pepper

1 Slice the leeks in half lengthways, wash them well and then slice evenly. Heat the stock to simmering point.

2 Heat the oil in a large pan and cook the garlic for 1 minute. Add the leeks, mushrooms and plenty of seasoning and cook over medium heat for about 10 minutes, or until the leeks have softened and browned. Spoon into a bowl and set aside.

3 Add 25g/1oz/2 tbsp of the butter to the pan. As soon as it has melted, add the onion and cook over medium heat for 5 minutes, until it has softened and is golden.

4 Stir in the rice and cook for about 1 minute until the grains begin to look translucent and are coated in the fat. Add a ladleful of stock and cook gently, stirring occasionally, until the liquid has been absorbed.

5 Continue to add stock, a ladleful at a time, stirring constantly, until all of it has been absorbed. This should take about 25–30 minutes. The risotto should be creamy and the rice should be tender but still al dente.

6 Just before serving, add the leeks and mushrooms, with the remaining butter. Stir in the grated lemon rind and juice. Add the Parmesan and herbs. Taste for seasoning before serving.

Risotto-stuffed Aubergines with Spicy Tomato Sauce

Glossy, purple aubergines from the south of Italy are wonderful filled with a rice stuffing, then baked with a cheese and pine nut topping.

Serves 4
4 small aubergines (eggplants)
105ml/7 tbsp olive oil
1 small onion, chopped
175g/6oz/scant 1 cup risotto rice
750ml/1¼ pints/3 cups
  vegetable stock

15ml/1 tbsp white wine vinegar
25g/1oz/¹⁄₃ cup freshly grated
  Parmesan cheese
15g/½oz/2 tbsp pine nuts

For the tomato sauce
300ml/½ pint/1¼ cups thick
  passata or puréed tomatoes
5ml/1 tsp mild curry paste
pinch of salt

1 Preheat the oven to 200°C/400°F/Gas 6. Cut the aubergines in half lengthways and remove the flesh with a small knife. Brush the shells with 30ml/2 tbsp of the oil and bake on a baking sheet, supported by crumpled foil, for 6–8 minutes.

2 Chop the aubergine flesh. Heat the remaining oil in a medium pan. Add the aubergine flesh and the onion, and cook over gentle heat for 3–4 minutes, until soft. Add the rice and stock, and leave to simmer, uncovered, for about 15 minutes. Stir in the the vinegar.

3 Increase the oven temperature to 230°C/450°F/Gas 8. Carefully spoon the rice mixture into the aubergine skins, top with the cheese and pine nuts, return to the oven and brown for 5 minutes.

4 To make the tomato sauce, mix the passata or puréed tomatoes with the curry paste in a small pan. Heat through and add salt to taste.

5 Spoon the tomato sauce on to four individual plates and arrange two aubergine halves on each one.

Energy 478Kcal/1985kJ; Fat 28.9g; Saturated Fat 7g; Carbohydrate 41.3g; Fibre 3.5g

Energy 606Kcal/2522kJ; Fat 26.2g; Saturated Fat 13.2g; Carbohydrate 77.7g; Fibre 2.9g

Mussel Risotto

Fresh root ginger and coriander add a distinctive flavour to this dish, while chillies give it a little heat.

Serves 3–4
900g/2lb fresh mussels, in
   their shells
about 250ml/8fl oz/1 cup dry
   white wine
30ml/2 tbsp olive oil
1 onion, chopped
2 garlic cloves, crushed
1–2 fresh green chillies, seeded
   and finely sliced
2.5cm/1in piece of fresh root
   ginger, grated
275g/10oz/1½ cups risotto rice
900ml/1½ pints/3¾ cups
   simmering fish stock
30ml/2 tbsp chopped fresh
   coriander (cilantro)
30ml/2 tbsp double (heavy) cream
salt and ground black pepper

1 Scrub the mussels; discard any that do not close when tapped. Place in a large pan. Add 120ml/4fl oz/½ cup of the wine and bring to the boil. Cover and cook for 4–5 minutes, until they have opened, shaking the pan occasionally. Drain, reserving the liquid; discard any unopened mussels. Remove the mussels from their shells, reserving a few in their shells. Strain the mussel liquid.

2 Heat the oil and fry the onion and garlic for 3–4 minutes, until beginning to soften. Add the chillies. Continue to cook over low heat for 1–2 minutes, stirring frequently, then stir in the ginger and fry gently for 1 minute more.

3 Add the rice and cook over a medium heat for 2 minutes, stirring, until the rice is coated in oil and becomes translucent. Stir in the reserved mussel liquid. When absorbed, add the remaining wine and cook, stirring, until this has been absorbed. Add the hot fish stock, a little at a time, making sure each addition has been absorbed before adding the next.

4 When the rice is three-quarters cooked, stir in the mussels. Add the coriander and season. Continue adding stock to the risotto until it is creamy and the rice is al dente. Remove from the heat, stir in the cream, cover and leave to rest for a few minutes. Spoon into a warmed serving dish, decorate with the reserved mussels in their shells and serve immediately.

Energy 439Kcal/1833kJ; Fat 11.3g; Saturated Fat 3.5g; Carbohydrate 56.6g; Fibre 0.2g

Seafood Risotto

You can use any shellfish or seafood for this risotto, as long as the total weight is similar to that used here.

Serves 4–6
450g/1lb fresh mussels, in
   their shells
about 250ml/8fl oz/1 cup dry
   white wine
225g/8oz sea bass fillet, skinned
   and cut into pieces
seasoned flour, for dusting
60ml/4 tbsp olive oil
8 scallops with corals separated,
   white parts halved or sliced
225g/8oz squid, cleaned and cut
   into rings
12 large raw prawns (shrimp) or
   langoustines, heads removed
2 shallots, finely chopped
1 garlic clove, crushed
400g/14oz/2 cups risotto rice
3 tomatoes, peeled, seeded
   and chopped
1.5 litres/2½ pints/6¼ cups
   simmering fish stock
30ml/2 tbsp chopped
   fresh parsley
30ml/2 tbsp double
   (heavy) cream
salt and ground black pepper

1 Scrub the mussels, discarding any that do not close when sharply tapped. Place in a large pan and add 90ml/6 tbsp of the wine. Bring to the boil, cover the pan and cook for 3–4 minutes, until all the mussels have opened, shaking the pan occasionally. Drain, reserving the liquid; discard any mussels that have not opened. Reserve a few mussels in their shells for garnishing; remove the rest from their shells. Strain the cooking liquid.

2 Dust the pieces of sea bass in seasoned flour. Heat 30ml/2 tbsp of the olive oil in a frying pan and fry the fish for 3–4 minutes, until cooked. Transfer to a plate. Add a little more oil to the pan and fry the white parts of the scallops for 1–2 minutes on both sides, until tender. Transfer to a plate.

3 Fry the squid for 3–4 minutes in the same pan, adding a little more oil if necessary, then set aside. Lastly, add the prawns and fry for a further 3–4 minutes, turning frequently until pink. Towards the end of cooking, add about 30ml/2 tbsp wine and continue cooking until the prawns are tender, but do not burn. Remove the prawns from the pan. When cool enough to handle, remove the shells and legs, leaving the tails intact.

4 In a large pan, heat the remaining olive oil and fry the shallots and garlic for 3–4 minutes over gentle heat until the shallots are soft. Add the rice and cook for a few minutes, stirring, until the rice is coated with oil and the grains are slightly translucent. Stir in the tomatoes, with the reserved liquid from the mussels.

5 When all the free liquid has been absorbed, add the remaining wine, stirring constantly. When it has also been absorbed, gradually add the hot stock, one ladleful at a time, continuing to stir the rice constantly and waiting until each quantity of stock has been absorbed before adding the next.

6 When the risotto is three-quarters cooked, carefully stir in all the seafood, except the mussels reserved for the garnish. Continue to cook until all the stock has been absorbed and the rice is tender but is still al dente. Stir in the parsley and cream and taste for seasoning. Cover the pan and leave the risotto to stand for 2–3 minutes. Serve, garnished with reserved mussels.

Energy 541Kcal/2265kJ; Fat 13.9g; Saturated Fat 3.5g; Carbohydrate 58.8g; Fibre 0.6g

Squid Risotto with Chilli

Tender squid is delicious in this exotic risotto.

Serves 3–4

about 450g/1lb squid, cleaned and cut into rings
about 45ml/3 tbsp olive oil
15g/½oz/1 tbsp butter
1 onion, finely chopped
2 garlic cloves, crushed
1 fresh red chilli, seeded and sliced
275g/10oz/1½ cups risotto rice
175ml/6fl oz/¾ cup dry white wine
1 litre/1¾ pints/4 cups simmering fish stock
30ml/2 tbsp chopped fresh coriander (cilantro)
salt and ground black pepper

For the marinade

2 ripe kiwi fruit, mashed
1 fresh red chilli, seeded and sliced
30ml/2 tbsp fresh lime juice

1 Mash the kiwi fruit for the marinade in a bowl, then stir in the chilli and lime juice. Add the squid, stirring to coat all the strips in the mixture. Season with salt and pepper, cover with clear film (plastic wrap) and chill for 4 hours or overnight.

2 Drain the squid. Heat 15ml/1 tbsp of the olive oil in a frying pan and cook the strips, in batches if necessary, for 30–60 seconds over high heat; cook them very quickly. Transfer to a plate and set aside. If too much juice accumulates in the pan, reserve it in a jug and add add more olive oil to the pan.

3 Heat the remaining oil with the butter in a large pan and gently fry the onion and garlic for 5–6 minutes, until soft. Add the sliced chilli to the pan and fry for 1 minute more.

4 Add the rice. Cook for a few minutes, stirring, until the rice is coated with oil and is slightly translucent, then stir in the wine until it has been absorbed. Gradually add the hot stock and the squid cooking liquid, a ladleful at a time, stirring and waiting until each quantity has been absorbed before adding the next.

5 When the rice is three-quarters cooked, stir in the squid and continue cooking the risotto until all the stock has been absorbed and the rice is tender. Season. Stir in the coriander, cover and leave to stand for a few minutes before serving.

Energy 460Kcal/1924kJ; Fat 10.9g; Saturated Fat 1.6g; Carbohydrate 59.9g; Fibre 0.5g

Scallop Risotto

Try to buy fresh scallops for this dish, as they taste much better than frozen ones. Fresh scallops come with the coral attached, which adds flavour and colour.

Serves 3–4

about 12 shelled scallops, with their corals
1 litre/1¾ pints/4 cups fish stock
50g/2oz/¼ cup butter
15ml/1 tbsp olive oil
30ml/2 tbsp Pernod
2 shallots, finely chopped
275g/10oz/1½ cups risotto rice
generous pinch of saffron threads, dissolved in 15ml/1 tbsp warm milk
30ml/2 tbsp chopped fresh parsley
60ml/4 tbsp double (heavy) cream
salt and ground black pepper

1 Separate the scallops from their corals. Cut the white flesh in half or into 2cm/¾in slices. Heat the stock until simmering.

2 Melt half the butter with 5ml/1 tsp oil. Fry the white parts of the scallops for 2–3 minutes. Pour over the Pernod, heat for a few seconds, then ignite and allow to flame for a few seconds. When the flames have died down, remove pan from the heat.

3 Heat the remaining butter and olive oil in another pan and fry the shallots for about 3–4 minutes, until soft but not browned. Add the rice and cook for a few minutes, stirring, until the rice is coated with oil and is beginning to turn translucent.

4 Gradually add the hot stock, a ladleful at a time, stirring constantly and waiting for each ladleful of stock to be absorbed before adding the next.

5 When the rice is very nearly cooked, add the scallops and all the juices from the pan, together with the corals, saffron milk, parsley and seasoning. Stir well to mix. Continue cooking, adding the remaining stock and stirring occasionally, until the risotto is thick and creamy.

6 Remove from the heat, stir in the cream and cover. Leave the risotto to stand for about 3 minutes before serving.

Energy 550Kcal/2290kJ; Fat 22.5g; Saturated Fat 12.2g; Carbohydrate 58.9g; Fibre 0.2g

Shellfish Risotto with Mixed Mushrooms

A quick and easy risotto, where all the liquid is added in one go. The method is well-suited to this shellfish dish, as it means everything cooks together undisturbed.

Serves 6

225g/8oz fresh mussels, in their shells
225g/8oz fresh Venus or carpet shell clams, in their shells
1.75 litres/3 pints/7½ cups chicken or vegetable stock
45ml/3 tbsp olive oil
1 onion, chopped
450g/1lb/2⅓ cups risotto rice
150ml/¼ pint/⅔ cup dry white wine
225g/8oz/2–3 cups assorted wild and cultivated mushrooms, trimmed and sliced
115g/4oz raw peeled prawns (shrimp), deveined
1 medium or 2 small squid, cleaned and sliced
3 drops truffle oil (optional)
75ml/5 tbsp chopped mixed fresh parsley and chervil
celery salt and cayenne pepper

1 Scrub the mussels and clams clean, discarding any that are open and do not close when tapped with a knife. Set aside.

2 Heat the stock and leave simmering until needed. Heat the oil in a large frying pan and fry the onion for 6–8 minutes, until soft but not browned.

3 Add the rice, stirring to coat the grains in oil, then pour in the stock and wine and cook for 5 minutes. Add the mushrooms and cook for 5 minutes more, stirring occasionally.

4 Add the prawns, squid, mussels and clams and stir into the rice. Cover the pan and simmer over low heat for 15 minutes, until the prawns have turned pink and the mussels and clams have opened. Discard any of the shellfish that remain closed.

5 Switch off the heat. Add the truffle oil, if using, and stir in the herbs. Cover tightly and leave to stand for 5–10 minutes to allow all the flavours to blend. Season to taste with celery salt and a pinch of cayenne and serve immediately.

Energy 423Kcal/1768kJ; Fat 7.5g; Saturated Fat 1.2g; Carbohydrate 62.5g; Fibre 0.6g

Risotto with Prawns

A dash of tomato purée gives this delicate prawn risotto a soft pink colour.

Serves 3–4

350g/12oz large raw prawns (shrimp), in their shells
1 bay leaf
1–2 fresh parsley sprigs
5ml/1 tsp whole peppercorns
2 garlic cloves, peeled and left whole
65g/2½oz/5 tbsp butter
2 shallots, finely chopped
275g/10oz/1½ cups risotto rice
15ml/1 tbsp tomato purée (paste), softened in 120ml/4fl oz/½ cup dry white wine
salt and ground black pepper

1 Put the prawns in a large pan with 1 litre/1¾ pints/4 cups water and the herbs, peppercorns and garlic. Bring to the boil over medium heat. As soon as the prawns turn pink, lift them out, peel them and return the shells to the pan. Boil the stock with the shells for a further 10 minutes, then strain. Return the stock to the clean pan and simmer gently until needed.

2 Slice the prawns in half lengthways, removing the dark vein along the back. Set four halves aside for the garnish, then roughly chop the rest.

3 Heat two-thirds of the butter in a flameproof casserole and fry the shallots until golden. Add the rice, mixing well to coat it with butter. Pour in the tomato purée and wine and cook until it has been absorbed. Add a ladleful of the simmering stock and stir until the stock has been absorbed.

4 Gradually add the remaining stock, a ladleful at a time, allowing the rice to absorb the liquid before adding more, and stirring constantly.

5 After 20–25 minutes, when all the stock has been absorbed, the risotto is creamy and the rice is al dente, stir in the chopped prawns and the remaining butter. Season to taste with salt and pepper. Cover and allow the risotto rest for 3–4 minutes. Spoon into a serving bowl, garnish with the reserved prawns and serve.

Energy 457Kcal/1905kJ; Fat 14.3g; Saturated Fat 8.6g; Carbohydrate 55.7g; Fibre 0.1g

Truffle & Lobster Risotto

To capture the precious qualities of truffle, partner it with lobster and serve in a silky smooth risotto. Both truffle shavings and truffle oil are added towards the end of cooking to preserve their flavour.

Serves 4
1.2 litres/2 pints/5 cups chicken stock
50g/2oz/4 tbsp unsalted butter
1 onion, chopped
350g/12oz/1¾ cups risotto rice
1 fresh thyme sprig
150ml/¼ pint/⅔ cup dry white wine
1 freshly cooked lobster
45ml/3 tbsp chopped mixed fresh parsley and chervil
3–4 drops truffle oil
2 hard-boiled eggs, cut into wedges
1 fresh black or white truffle
salt and ground black pepper

1 Heat the stock and keep at a gentle simmer until needed. Melt the butter in a pan, add the onion and fry until the onion is soft. Add the rice and stir well to coat with fat.

2 Add the thyme, then pour in the wine and cook until it has been absorbed. Add the chicken stock a little at a time, stirring. Allow each ladleful to be absorbed before adding the next.

3 Twist off the lobster tail, cut the underside with scissors and remove the white tail meat. Carefully break open the claws with a small kitchen hammer and remove the flesh. Cut half the meat into big chunks, then roughly chop the remainder.

4 Stir in the chopped lobster meat, half the chopped herbs and the truffle oil. Remove the rice from the heat, cover and leave to stand for 5 minutes. Divide among plates and top with the lobster chunks and hard-boiled eggs. To serve, shave fresh truffle over each portion and sprinkle with the remaining herbs.

> **Cook's Tip**
> To make the most of the aromatic truffle scent, keep the tuber in a rice jar for a few days before use.

Energy 520Kcal/2172kJ; Fat 14.3g; Saturated Fat 7.4g; Carbohydrate 71.3g; Fibre 0.2g

Crab Risotto

A luxurious way to serve fresh crab, this dish is laced with Marsala and cream.

Serves 3–4
2 large cooked crabs
15ml/1 tbsp olive oil
25g/1oz/2 tbsp butter
2 shallots, finely chopped
275g/10oz/1½ cups risotto rice
75ml/5 tbsp Marsala or brandy
1 litre/1¾ pints/4 cups simmering fish stock
5ml/1 tsp chopped fresh tarragon
5ml/1 tsp chopped fresh parsley
60ml/4 tbsp double (heavy) cream
salt and ground black pepper

1 To remove the crabmeat, hold a crab firmly in one hand and hit the underside firmly with the heel of your hand to loosen the shell. Using your thumbs, push against the body and pull away from the shell. From the inside of the shell, remove and discard the intestines. Discard the grey gills – "dead man's fingers". Break off the claws and legs from the body, then use a small hammer or crackers to break them open. Using a pick, remove the meat from the claws and legs. Set the meat aside.

2 Using a pick or a skewer, pick out the white meat from the body cavities and add to the rest of the meat. Reserve some white meat to garnish. Scoop out the brown meat from inside the shell and set aside with the white meat.

3 Heat the oil and butter in a pan and gently fry the shallots until soft but not brown. Add the rice. Cook for a few minutes, stirring, until the rice is slightly translucent. Add the Marsala, bring to the boil and cook, stirring, until the liquid evaporates.

4 Add a ladleful of hot stock and cook, stirring, until all the stock has been absorbed. Continue cooking in this way until about two-thirds of the stock has been added, then carefully stir in all the crabmeat and the herbs.

5 Continue to cook the risotto, adding the remaining stock. When the rice is al dente, remove it from the heat, stir in the cream and taste for seasoning. Cover and leave to stand for 3 minutes. Serve garnished with the reserved white crabmeat.

Energy 496Kcal/2060kJ; Fat 18.7g; Saturated Fat 8.9g; Carbohydrate 56.4g; Fibre 0.2g

Monkfish Risotto

Monkfish is a versatile, firm-textured fish, ideal for cooking in a risotto.

Serves 3–4

about 450g/1lb monkfish, cut into cubes
seasoned flour, for coating
1 litre/1¾ pints/4 cups fish stock
30ml/2 tbsp olive oil
40g/1½oz/3 tbsp butter
2 shallots, finely chopped
1 lemon grass stalk, finely chopped
275g/10oz/1½ cups risotto rice, preferably Carnaroli
175ml/6fl oz/¾ cup dry white wine
30ml/2 tbsp chopped fresh parsley
salt and white pepper
dressed salad leaves, to serve

1 Place the monkfish cubes in a bowl and toss in seasoned flour until coated. Heat the stock in a pan and leave to simmer gently until needed.

2 Heat 15ml/1 tbsp of the oil with half the butter in a frying pan. Fry the monkfish cubes over medium to high heat for 3–4 minutes, until cooked, turning occasionally. Transfer to a plate and set aside.

3 Heat the remaining oil and butter in a pan and fry the shallots over low heat for about 4 minutes, until soft but not brown. Add the lemon grass and cook for 1–2 minutes more.

4 Add the rice. Cook for 2–3 minutes, stirring, until the rice is coated with oil and is slightly translucent. Gradually add the wine and the hot stock, stirring and waiting until each ladleful has been absorbed before adding the next.

5 When the rice is about three-quarters cooked, stir in the monkfish. Continue to cook the risotto, adding the remaining stock and stirring constantly until the grains of rice are tender, but still al dente. Season with salt and white pepper.

6 Remove the pan from the heat, stir in the parsley and cover with the lid. Leave the risotto to stand for a few minutes before serving with a garnish of dressed salad leaves.

Salmon Risotto with Cucumber & Tarragon

This simple risotto is cooked all in one go, and is easier to make than the traditional version.

Serves 4

1.2 litres/2 pints/5 cups chicken or fish stock
25g/1oz/2 tbsp butter
small bunch of spring onions (scallions), white parts only, chopped
½ cucumber, peeled, seeded and chopped
350g/12oz/1¾ cups risotto rice
150ml/¼ pint/⅔ cup dry white wine
450g/1lb salmon fillet, skinned and diced
45ml/3 tbsp chopped fresh tarragon
salt and ground black pepper

1 Heat the stock in a pan and keep at a gentle simmer. Melt the butter in a large pan and add the spring onions and cucumber. Cook for 2–3 minutes, stirring frequently, without allowing the spring onions to colour.

2 Stir in the rice, then pour in the stock and wine. Bring to the boil, then lower the heat and simmer, uncovered, for 10 minutes, stirring occasionally.

3 Stir in the diced salmon and season to taste with salt and black pepper. Continue cooking for a further 5 minutes, stirring occasionally, then switch off the heat. Cover and leave to stand for 5 minutes.

4 Remove the lid, add the chopped tarragon and mix lightly. Spoon into a warmed serving bowl and serve.

> **Cook's Tip**
> If you prefer to cook the traditional way, add the liquid gradually, adding the salmon about two-thirds of the way through cooking. Carnaroli risotto rice would be best for this recipe.

Energy 431Kcal/1802kJ; Fat 9.1g; Saturated Fat 5.3g; Carbohydrate 56.5g; Fibre 0.3g

Energy 594Kcal/2477kJ; Fat 18.1g; Saturated Fat 5.4g; Carbohydrate 70.9g; Fibre 0.4g

Risotto with Bacon, Baby Courgettes & Peppers

A medley of colours, this creamy vegetable risotto would make a perfect light lunch or dinner, served with chunks of rustic bread and a glass of dry white wine.

Serves 4
30ml/2 tbsp olive oil
115g/4oz rindless streaky (fatty) bacon rashers (strips), cut into thick strips
1.2 litres/2 pints/5 cups vegetable or chicken stock
350g/12oz/1¾ cups risotto rice
30ml/2 tbsp single (light) cream
45ml/3 tbsp dry sherry
50g/2oz/⅔ cup freshly grated Parmesan cheese
50g/2oz/⅔ cup chopped fresh parsley
salt and ground black pepper

For the vegetables
1 small red (bell) pepper, seeded
1 small green (bell) pepper, seeded
25g/1oz/2 tbsp butter
75g/3oz horse mushrooms, sliced
225g/8oz baby courgettes (zucchini), halved
1 onion, halved and sliced
1 garlic clove, crushed

1 Heat half the oil in a frying pan. Add the bacon and heat gently until the fat runs. Increase the heat and fry until crisp, then drain on kitchen paper and set aside. Heat the stock in a pan and leave to simmer gently until required.

2 Heat the remaining oil in a heavy pan over medium heat. Add the rice, stir to coat the grains, then ladle in a little of the hot stock. Stir until it has been absorbed. Gradually add the rest of the stock in the same way, stirring constantly.

3 To prepare the vegetables, cut the peppers into chunks. Melt the butter in a separate pan and fry the peppers, mushrooms, courgettes, onion and garlic until the onion is just tender. Season well with salt and pepper, then stir in the bacon.

4 When all the stock has been absorbed by the rice, stir in the cream, sherry, Parmesan, parsley and seasoning. Spoon on to individual plates and top with the vegetables and bacon.

Risotto with Smoked Bacon & Tomato

A classic risotto, with plenty of onions, smoked bacon and sun-dried tomatoes. You'll want to keep going back for more!

Serves 4–6
8 sun-dried tomatoes in olive oil
1 litre/1¾ pints/4 cups vegetable stock
275g/10oz rindless smoked back bacon, cut into 2.5cm/1in pieces
75g/3oz/6 tbsp butter
450g/1lb onions, roughly chopped
2 garlic cloves, crushed
350g/12oz/1¾ cups risotto rice
300ml/½ pint/1¼ cups dry white wine
50g/2oz/⅔ cup freshly grated Parmesan cheese
45ml/3 tbsp mixed chopped fresh chives and flat leaf parsley
salt and ground black pepper

1 Drain the sun-dried tomatoes and reserve 15ml/1 tbsp of the oil. Roughly chop the tomatoes and set aside. Heat the stock in a pan and leave to simmer gently until required.

2 Heat the oil from the sun-dried tomatoes in a large pan and fry the bacon until well cooked and golden. Remove with a slotted spoon and drain on kitchen paper.

3 Melt 25g/1oz/2 tbsp of the butter in a pan and fry the onions and garlic over medium heat for 10 minutes, until soft and golden brown. Stir in the rice. Cook for 1 minute, until the grains turn translucent. Stir the wine into the stock. Add a ladleful of the mixture to the rice and cook gently, stirring, until the liquid has been absorbed.

4 Stir in another ladleful of the stock and wine mixture and allow it to be absorbed. Repeat this process until all the liquid has been used up. This should take 25–30 minutes. The risotto will turn thick and creamy, and the rice should be al dente.

5 Just before serving, stir in the bacon, sun-dried tomatoes, Parmesan, half the herbs and the remaining butter. Add salt and pepper to taste and serve sprinkled with the remaining herbs.

Energy 624Kcal/2595kJ; Fat 24.2g; Saturated Fat 10g; Carbohydrate 78.4g; Fibre 3g

Energy 507Kcal/2110kJ; Fat 21.2g; Saturated Fat 11.1g; Carbohydrate 54.4g; Fibre 1.6g

Leek & Prosciutto Risotto

Flavoured with tasty Italian cured ham, this simple risotto makes an easy supper that is full of flavour.

Serves 3–4
1 litre/1¾ pints/4 cups
  chicken stock
7.5ml/1½ tsp olive oil
40g/1½oz/3 tbsp butter
2 leeks, cut in slices
175g/6oz prosciutto, torn
  into pieces
75g/3oz/generous 1 cup button
  (white) mushrooms, sliced
275g/10oz/1½ cups risotto rice
45ml/3 tbsp chopped fresh flat
  leaf parsley
40g/1½oz/½ cup freshly grated
  Parmesan cheese
salt and ground black pepper

1 Heat the stock in a pan and simmer gently until needed.

2 Heat the oil and butter in another pan and fry the leeks until soft. Set aside a few strips of prosciutto for the garnish and add the rest to the pan. Fry for 1 minute, then add the mushrooms and fry, stirring, for 2–3 minutes, until lightly browned.

3 Add the rice. Cook, stirring, for 1–2 minutes, until the grains are evenly coated in oil and have become translucent around the edges. Add a ladleful of hot stock. Stir until this has been absorbed completely, then add the next ladleful. Continue in this way until all the stock has been absorbed.

4 When the risotto is creamy and the rice is tender but still al dente, stir in the parsley and Parmesan. Taste for seasoning, remove from the heat and cover. Rest for a few minutes, then spoon into a bowl and garnish with the reserved prosciutto.

> **Cook's Tip**
> *Italy is well known for its prosciutto crudo, salted and air-dried ham. The most famous of these, prosciutto di Parma, comes from the area around Parma, where Parmesan cheese is also made. The pigs from this region are fed on the whey from the cheese-making process, which makes their flesh mild and sweet.*

Energy 444Kcal/1853kJ; Fat 14.8g; Saturated Fat 8g; Carbohydrate 58g; Fibre 2.1g

Risi e Bisi

A classic pea and ham risotto from the Veneto region, northern Italy. Traditionally this is served as an appetizer in Italy, but it also makes a fine light main course dish.

Serves 4
75g/3oz/6 tbsp butter
1 small onion, finely chopped
about 1 litre/1¾ pints/4 cups
  chicken stock
275g/10oz/1½ cups risotto rice
150ml/¼ pint/⅔ cup dry
  white wine
225g/8oz/2 cups frozen petits
  pois, thawed
115g/4oz cooked ham, diced
salt and ground black pepper
50g/2oz/⅔ cup freshly grated
  Parmesan cheese, to serve

1 Heat the stock in a pan and keep at a gentle simmer until needed. Melt 50g/2oz/¼ cup of the butter in a pan until foaming. Add the onion and cook gently for about 3 minutes, stirring frequently, until softened.

2 Add the rice to the onion mixture. Stir until the grains start to swell, then pour in the wine. Stir until it stops sizzling and most of it has been absorbed, then pour in a little hot stock, with salt and pepper to taste. Stir continuously, over low heat, until all the stock has been absorbed.

3 Add the remaining stock, a ladleful at a time, allowing the rice to absorb the liquid before adding more, and stirring constantly. Add the peas after about 20 minutes. After 25–30 minutes, the rice should be al dente and the risotto moist and creamy.

4 Gently stir in the cooked ham and the remaining butter. Heat through until the butter has melted, then taste for seasoning. Transfer to a warmed serving bowl. Grate or shave a little Parmesan over the top and serve the rest separately.

> **Cook's Tip**
> *Always use fresh Parmesan cheese, grated off a block. It has a far superior flavour to ready-grated Parmesan.*

Energy 551Kcal/2290kJ; Fat 21.7g; Saturated Fat 12.8g; Carbohydrate 63g; Fibre 2.9g

Rabbit & Lemon Grass Risotto

The addition of exotic lemon grass adds a pleasant tang to this country risotto.

Serves 3–4
225g/8oz rabbit meat
seasoned flour, for coating
50g/2oz/¼ cup butter
15ml/1 tbsp olive oil
45ml/3 tbsp dry sherry
1 litre/1¾ pints/4 cups
　chicken stock
1 onion, finely chopped
1 garlic clove, crushed
1 lemon grass stalk, peeled and
　very finely sliced
275g/10oz/1½ cups risotto rice,
　preferably Carnaroli
10ml/2 tsp finely chopped
　fresh thyme
45ml/3 tbsp double (heavy) cream
25g/1oz/⅓ cup freshly grated
　Parmesan cheese
salt and ground black pepper

1 Cut the rabbit into strips and coat in the seasoned flour. Heat half the butter and oil in a frying pan and fry the rabbit quickly until evenly brown. Add the sherry and allow to boil briefly to burn off the alcohol. Season with salt and pepper and set aside.

2 Pour the stock into a pan and simmer gently until required.

3 Heat the remaining olive oil and butter in a large pan. Fry the onion and garlic over low heat for 4–5 minutes, until the onion is soft. Add the lemon grass and cook for a few minutes.

4 Add the rice and stir to coat in the oil. Add a ladleful of stock and cook, stirring, until the liquid has been absorbed. Continue adding the stock in this way, stirring constantly. When the rice is almost cooked, stir in three-quarters of the rabbit strips, with the pan juices. Add the thyme and seasoning.

5 Continue cooking until the rice is tender but is still al dente. Stir in the cream and Parmesan, remove from the heat and cover. Leave to stand before serving, garnished with rabbit strips.

> **Cook's Tip**
> *If rabbit is not available, use chicken or turkey instead.*

Energy 477Kcal/1981kJ; Fat 21.9g; Saturated Fat 13.6g; Carbohydrate 56.2g; Fibre 0.2g

Duck Risotto

Brandy-flavoured duck is enhanced with orange in this spectacular risotto.

Serves 3–4
2 duck breasts
30ml/2 tbsp brandy
30ml/2 tbsp orange juice
15ml/1 tbsp olive oil (optional)
1 onion, finely chopped
1 garlic clove, crushed
275g/10oz/1½ cups risotto rice
1–1.2 litres/1¾–2 pints/4–5 cups
　hot duck or chicken stock
5ml/1 tsp chopped fresh thyme
5ml/1 tsp chopped fresh mint
10ml/2 tsp grated orange rind
40g/1½oz/½ cup freshly grated
　Parmesan cheese
salt and ground black pepper
strips of thinly pared orange rind,
　to garnish

1 Score the skin of the duck breasts and rub with salt. Fry, skin-side down, in a heavy frying pan and dry-fry over medium heat for 6–8 minutes to render the fat. Transfer to a plate and discard the skin. Cut into strips about 2cm/¾in wide.

2 Pour all but 15ml/1 tbsp of the rendered duck fat from the pan into a cup, then reheat the fat in the pan. Fry the duck slices for 2–3 minutes over medium high heat, until evenly brown but not overcooked. Add the brandy, heat to simmering point and then ignite. When the flames have died down, add the orange juice and season. Remove from the heat; set aside.

3 In a pan, heat either 15ml/1 tbsp of the remaining duck fat or use olive oil. Fry the onion and garlic over gentle heat, until the onion is soft but not browned. Add the rice and cook, stirring all the time, until the grains are coated in oil and have become slightly translucent around the edges.

4 Add the stock, a ladleful at a time, waiting for each quantity to be absorbed completely before adding the next. Just before adding the final ladleful of stock, stir in the duck, with the thyme and mint. Cook until the risotto is creamy and the rice al dente.

5 Add the orange rind and Parmesan. Taste for seasoning, then remove from the heat, cover the pan and leave to stand for a few minutes. Serve garnished with orange rind.

Energy 408Kcal/1708kJ; Fat 8.5g; Saturated Fat 3g; Carbohydrate 56.7g; Fibre 0.2g

Chicken Liver Risotto

The combination of chicken livers, bacon, parsley and thyme gives this risotto a wonderfully rich flavour.

Serves 2–4
175g/6oz chicken livers
900ml–1 litre/1½–1¾ pints/
    3¾–4 cups chicken stock
about 15ml/1 tbsp olive oil
about 25g/1oz/2 tbsp butter
about 40g/1½oz speck or 3
    strips (rashers) of rindless
bacon, finely chopped
2 shallots, finely chopped
1 garlic clove, crushed
1 celery stick, finely sliced
275g/10oz/1½ cups risotto rice
175ml/6fl oz/¾ cup dry
    white wine
5ml/1 tsp chopped fresh thyme
15ml/1 tbsp chopped parsley
salt and ground black pepper
parsley and thyme sprigs,
    to garnish

1 Clean the chicken livers carefully, removing any fat or membrane. Rinse well, pat dry with kitchen paper and cut into small, even pieces. Heat the stock and simmer until needed.

2 Heat the oil and butter in a frying pan and fry the speck or bacon for 2–3 minutes. Add the shallots, garlic and celery and continue frying for 3–4 minutes over low heat, until the vegetables are slightly softened. Increase the heat and add the chicken livers, stir-frying for a few minutes, until they are brown.

3 Add the rice. Cook, stirring, for a few minutes, then pour over the wine. Allow to boil, stirring frequently, taking care not to break up the chicken livers. When all the wine has been absorbed, add the hot stock, a ladleful at a time, stirring.

4 About halfway through cooking, add the thyme and season with salt and pepper. Continue to add the stock as before, making sure that it is absorbed before adding more.

5 When the risotto is creamy and the rice is tender but al dente, stir in the parsley. Taste for seasoning. Remove the pan from the heat, cover and leave to stand for a few minutes before serving, garnished with parsley and thyme.

Energy 418Kcal/1742kJ; Fat 11.6g; Saturated Fat 4.8g; Carbohydrate 55.8g; Fibre 0.2g

Risotto with Chicken

This is a classic combination of chicken and rice, cooked with prosciutto, white wine and Parmesan cheese.

Serves 6
1.75 litres/3 pints/7½ cups
    chicken stock
30ml/2 tbsp olive oil
225g/8oz skinless chicken breast
    fillets, cut into 2.5cm/1in cubes
1 onion, finely chopped
1 garlic clove, finely chopped
450g/1lb/2⅓ cups risotto rice
120ml/4fl oz/½ cup dry
    white wine
1.5ml/¼ tsp saffron threads
50g/2oz prosciutto, cut into
    thin strips
25g/1oz/2 tbsp butter, cubed
25g/1oz/⅓ cup freshly grated
    Parmesan cheese, plus extra
    to serve
salt and ground black pepper
flat leaf parsley, to garnish

1 Heat the stock in a pan and simmer gently until needed. Heat the oil in a frying pan over medium-high heat. Add the chicken cubes and cook, stirring, until they start to turn white.

2 Reduce the heat to low and add the onion and garlic. Cook, stirring, until the onion is soft. Stir in the rice. Sauté for 1–2 minutes, stirring constantly, until all the rice grains are coated.

3 Add the wine and bubble, stirring, until the wine has been absorbed. Stir the saffron into the simmering stock, then add ladlefuls of stock to the rice, allowing each ladleful to be absorbed before adding the next.

4 When the rice is three-quarters cooked, add the prosciutto and continue cooking until the rice is just tender and the risotto creamy. Add the butter and the Parmesan and stir in well. Season with salt and pepper to taste. Serve the risotto hot, sprinkled with more Parmesan, and garnish with parsley.

> **Cook's Tip**
> *Try turkey for a modern version of this classic recipe.*

Energy 418kcal/1744kJ; Fat 9.5g; Saturated Fat 3.8g; Carbohydrate 60.9g; Fibre 0.1g

Index